MAKING PEACE

MAKING PEACE

by

George J. Mitchell

Alfred A. Knopf

NEW YORK

1999

THIS IS A BORZOI BOOK
PUBLISHED BY ALFRED A. KNOPF, INC.

Copyright © 1999 by George J. Mitchell

ISBN 0-375-40606-9
LC 99-61004

For my wife, Heather, and my son, Andrew,
and for his sixty-one friends in Northern Ireland

Contents

Preface

THIS is not a history of Northern Ireland, nor is it a history of the negotiations which led to the Good Friday Agreement. Rather, this is a personal account of my experiences in Northern Ireland. I have included accounts of other events as I needed to provide a clearer context and meaning.

From February 1995 through May 1998 I spent most of my time going to, coming from, and working in Northern Ireland. It was the most difficult task I have ever undertaken, far more demanding than the six years I served as majority leader of the United States Senate. But it was well worth the effort; the outcome was the most gratifying event of my public life.

Northern Ireland is a captivating land of great natural beauty, of green fields and rolling hills. It is a land well watered by oceans, rivers, and loughs, rain, mist, and fog. It is inhabited by shrewd and hardy people who are energetic, articulate, tough, and pragmatic. They have inflicted terrible suffering on one another. Their history includes a litany of vicious beatings, brutal murders, and devastating bombings. For a long time death, destruction, and maiming were routine. The well-attended, highly emotional funeral was a part of the social fabric.

Perhaps because the people have seen so much death, they love life. They are warm and generous and they have an earthy sense of humor. They love to eat and drink, and they love to talk even more; how they love to talk! I have been told that I'm a good listener; I got plenty of practice in Northern Ireland. For the two years of negotiations, I listened and listened, and then I listened some more. At times it was interesting, at times entertaining; it was also often repetitive, frustrating, and deliberately quarrelsome.

Once among the people of Northern Ireland, I became increasingly fond of them. I can never be one of them, of course, but I enjoyed enough of their laughter and shared enough of their grief that I feel very close to them.

I am an American, proud to be a citizen of what I believe to be the most open, the most free, the most just society in human history. But a large part of my heart will forever be in Northern Ireland.

MAKING PEACE

"I have never known peace."

I am afraid.
Afraid of the land that I live in,
That I was born in.
The ground I tread each day
Resounds with shots,
With screams;
It is saturated with tears,
Tears that have never ceased flowing.
I have never known peace.

Excerpted from a poem entitled "No Hope For Tomorrow,"
written during the Troubles by Karyn Woods of Northern Ireland
when she was fourteen years old.

THE telephone in my office rang at 4:45 p.m. David Trimble was on the line. This was the call I'd been waiting for. That morning we had distributed the final version of the agreement to the British and Irish governments and the eight Northern Ireland political parties, which were involved in the negotiations to end the conflict. Throughout the day I had been talking with the leaders of the parties. How's it going? Have you been through the agreement? What do you think? What do your people think? Can you vote for it? When can I set the meeting to vote on it? I tried to answer their questions, to ease their doubts. I was very tired, but I had to be wide awake for this, the last day, a day of questioning, exhorting, pleading.

Gradually the leaders responded. Some were enthusiastic, others restrained but positive. By four o'clock I had heard from both governments and seven of the parties, all of whom were prepared to support the agreement.

Only the Ulster Unionists remained. Theirs was the largest and most important of the unionist parties, so their vote would be decisive. Under the complex voting procedure governing the negotiations, the Ulster Unionists were one of four participants who had veto power. If they said no, the agreement was dead, the peace process over. Twenty-two months of negotiations were about to end—and I still didn't know how.

The Ulster Unionists had been in a closed meeting all afternoon, and the rumors were flying: Their delegates were badly divided, shouting at one another; they were working it out. They were against it; they were for it. David Trimble, their leader, was in control; Trimble had lost control. The meeting would be over soon; it could go on all day.

I could no longer tell fact from fiction, reality from rumor. So I waited, tired and nervous, thinking about how to deal with a no vote from the Ulster Unionists. I didn't have to worry about a yes vote. That would be easy to handle. But a no would have profound adverse consequences. Many more people could die.

I had been involved in the peace process in Northern Ireland for more than three years, the last twenty-two months as chairman of the negotiations. It had all come down to this last call from Trimble. An agreement could mean peace after centuries of conflict and decades of war, during which thousands had been killed and tens of thousands injured. An agreement could save so many lives, give hope to so many people. Failure could mean more years of war, more death, more destruction, more despair. After so much effort it would be a crushing letdown.

I took a deep breath and picked up the phone.

"Hello, David."

"Hello, George."

"How's it going?"

"We're ready."

"Are you all right?"

"We're ready to do the business."

"That's great. Congratulations."

"Thank you."

"I'd like to call the meeting as soon as possible. Can you be ready in fifteen minutes?"

"Yes."

"I'd like it to be a short meeting. No long speeches. Let's get to a vote right away. Everyone can talk as long as they want afterward."

"That's fine with me."

"I'll see you at five."

I took a deep breath and felt tears welling in my eyes—tears of exhaustion, tears of relief, tears of joy. I had to sit down.

As majority leader of the United States Senate, I had learned that when you've got the votes, you vote. Delay can only hurt. After long and difficult negotiations, the votes were there for the agreement. I was determined that they be cast as soon as possible. I didn't want to take a chance on a last-minute change of mind. I instructed my staff to notify the governments and the leaders of the other parties that there would be a formal session of all of the negotiators at five o'clock, and that I wanted a short meeting and an early vote.

I had only a few minutes to prepare. But first I had to close my eyes, to calm down, to collect my thoughts. It was Friday, April 10, 1998, Good Friday. I was totally exhausted. I had been awake for nearly thirty-six hours, in meetings almost continuously since early Thursday morning. And for most of the preceding week I had slept only a few hours a night.

But despite the exhaustion, I felt an exhilarating surge of accomplishment. We had done it. After seemingly endless negotiations, an agreement was within reach. What had seemed impossible for so long was about to happen. I could hardly believe it.

Then my thoughts shifted. I had promised my wife, Heather, that I would be home for Easter, to take her and our boy Andrew for a walk in Central Park. I pictured a warm spring day, me carrying my six-month-old son on a leisurely stroll across the large meadow in the park. I smiled and started to doze off.

Suddenly I sat up straight and my eyes popped open. It was three minutes to five. I still had to go in and chair the meeting, hold the vote, and announce the result. I got up, walked out of my office and down the hall, and entered the large meeting room, as I had done hundreds of times before. But this time was different. This was the last time. This time there would be an agreement.

Two governments and eight political parties were about to commit themselves to peace, political stability, and reconciliation in Northern Ireland.

My Irish journey was over.

CHAPTER 2

"Would you be willing to help?"

ALTHOUGH I didn't realize it at the time, my journey to Northern Ireland began in December 1982, when I decided that I would limit the time of my service in the United States Senate. I had been appointed to the Senate in May 1980 to complete the unexpired term of Edmund Muskie, who resigned to become secretary of state. His Senate term continued through 1982, giving me two and a half years to demonstrate to the people of Maine that I deserved election in my own right to a full six-year term. As it turned out, I needed every bit of that time.

Appointed senators rarely win election on their own, and it looked as though I would continue that tradition. Throughout 1980 and 1981, Maine's two members of the House of Representatives, both Republicans, jockeyed for position in what was widely perceived as the sure thing of defeating me. In May 1981 one of them, David Emery, released a public opinion poll which showed him trouncing me by 61 percent to 25 percent—a thirty-six-point spread. Not to be outdone, the other House member, Olympia Snowe, announced a poll which had her ahead of me by thirty-three points. Kenneth Curtis, a former governor, then stated that he was considering running against me in the Democratic primary. He cited yet another poll, showing him leading by twenty-two points.

Publication of the polls produced the intended and predictable result: an avalanche of negative news reports and a growing uneasiness among Democrats about the viability of my candidacy. I had been working hard for a year, but the only response to my political problems I could devise was to work even harder.

I had been traveling around the state, speaking at service clubs and high schools and going to bean suppers. But these were random appearances, usually in response to invitations I received. I now began a systematic effort to visit every service club, high school, hospital, grange hall, senior citizens center, and manufacturing facility in the state. Instead of eight to ten public events each weekend I attended twelve to fifteen. I also increased the time I devoted to researching and studying each issue on which the Senate voted.

It was an extremely difficult year. I was usually tired, often discouraged, always anxious. But I never felt that my situation was hopeless; I never lost faith in myself or my principles.

Over time, my prospects improved. Curtis decided, for health reasons, not to seek the nomination. Snowe deferred to Emery and withdrew from consideration. It was then Emery's bad luck that the incumbent Republican administration, and those candidates associated with it, were held responsible for the worsening economy. Late in the campaign the tide turned decisively in my favor. In the election I received 61 percent of the votes.

Among the lessons I learned from this experience were the importance of having a plan and sticking to it while retaining the flexibility to make adjustments as circumstances change; the necessity of total commitment; and the need for patience and perseverance to overcome the inevitable setbacks. These are not brilliant insights, but rather the kind of common sense that is often overwhelmed by panic at the first sign of adversity.

Shortly after the election I began to think seriously about my future in the Senate. I had seen many senators become totally consumed by the institution. I now realized that I had become one of them. I worked seven days a week, twelve to fourteen hours a day. My marriage suffered, my other interests atrophied. Since I had just received a sizeable majority of the vote after serving as an appointed senator for less than a full term, I was confident that with a full term I could establish myself so solidly that I could win re-election in the future. (My analysis was correct. In 1988 I received 81 percent of the vote, the highest percentage ever achieved by a candidate in a contested statewide election in Maine history.) But the more I thought about it, the more deeply I felt that I should not try to make the Senate a lifetime career. On Christmas Day, 1982, I decided to term-limit myself. It was a private decision. I kept it to myself for eleven years.

Just after Christmas in 1993, I decided that the time had come to leave the Senate. In late February 1994 I notified my staff and asked them to make preparations for a public announcement. March 5 was chosen as the date, Portland as the place.

On the morning of March 4, I videotaped a five-minute statement to be broadcast throughout Maine the next day. Although I ordinarily could do tapes on the first try, I needed three takes for this one. I found, to my surprise, that it was hard to say the words now, when it really counted, as opposed to when I had been just thinking about it. The final tape was barely acceptable, definitely not one of my best efforts.

That evening I went to the White House. By coincidence I had been invited to attend a small dinner in the First Family's living quarters, and I sat next to President Clinton. Near the end of the dinner I asked if I could speak to him privately for a few minutes. He suggested I join him in his study, where we talked for two and a half hours. The president was obviously surprised when I told him of my plans. He first tried to get me to change my mind. During the conversation he asked me, "If in the future something comes up where I think you can be of assistance, would you be willing to help? Or are you just turned off of politics?" I told him that I was not turned off, that I loved public service, and that I would be happy to help on anything he thought was important. He didn't mention Northern Ireland, and it never crossed my mind. But on that evening, without realizing it, I took the second step on my journey to Northern Ireland.

On November 1 President Clinton issued a statement on Northern Ireland. It was part of a continuing process under which, for the first time, the problems there were given a high priority by an American administration. In the statement he announced his intention to sponsor a White House Conference on Trade and Investment in Northern Ireland. It was to be part of a strategy to support the effort to bring peace to that troubled land by encouraging economic growth and job creation.

In early December I was asked by a member of the White House staff if I would undertake a diplomatic mission on behalf of the president. When I asked what it would involve, he said it would require all my time. I told him that wasn't possible. I was to be married on December 10 and was planning to return to private life. I was interested in doing something involving public policy, but I wasn't interested in anything that was a full-time job.

Later, I was shown the president's November 1 statement on Northern Ireland and was asked if I had any interest in getting involved there. Although I had never been to Northern Ireland, I was generally aware of the situation. I asked, "Is the president planning to appoint an envoy to Northern Ireland?" Not an envoy, I was told, because that was a sensitive subject with the British government. "But he does want someone to put together a trade conference in Washington in the spring. That would take just a few days of your time. Would you do it?" I said I would think about it and get back to him. I talked with friends at the State Department and on the National Security Council staff at the White House. I also discussed it with Heather. The task seemed interesting and undemanding, and it would be over in a few months, so later I called back and said I would take it on. I had taken the third step on my journey to Northern Ireland.

I left the Senate on January 2, 1995. Seven days later I was sworn in as the special advisor to the president and the secretary of state on economic initiatives in Ireland. The title was long and vague enough not to be offensive to the British government, or to anyone else. My mission was simple: organize a conference in Washington on trade and investment in Northern Ireland and the six counties in the Republic of Ireland which border on the north. I was given an office in the State Department and the authority to hire a small staff. I asked Martha Pope to join me. She had been a member of my Senate staff since 1981, rising to the position of chief of staff. I had then appointed her Senate sergeant at arms, the first woman to hold that position. She didn't know any more about Northern Ireland than I did, but I trusted her judgment and her integrity; in the years to come, both were to prove invaluable, to her, to me, and to the cause of peace in Northern Ireland. The State Department assigned David Pozorski to my staff. He was a career foreign service officer, insightful and methodical. For a brief time he served as acting U.S. consul in Belfast, and he knows the politicians and the issues there.

Later, when the negotiations began, I was joined by Kelly Currie, who had worked for a time on my Senate staff. He had left to attend law school and now practices with a large firm in New York. He took a leave of absence to spend two years in Belfast. He is intelligent and gets along very well with people. Pope, Pozorski, and Currie formed a dedicated, able staff, and they deserve a lot of credit for whatever effect I had on the peace process.

A month later I made my first trip to Northern Ireland. At the time I thought it would be my last, and I remember it vividly. I had lived in Berlin and was familiar with the Berlin Wall. But I had never heard of the "Peace Line." When I went to it for the first time, I was taken aback.

The Peace Line is a wall that stands up to thirty feet high, is topped in some places with barbed wire, and goes right through the middle of Belfast—through urban streets, even through buildings. It is one of the most depressing structures I've ever seen. To call it the Peace Line is a huge irony. The name, presumably, is born of the notion that peace can be achieved by building a wall between two warring communities, in this case unionists, who are predominantly Protestant, and nationalists, who are predominantly Catholic. Unfortunately, if people are determined enough, they can get around, through, and over a wall, and enough of them did so in Northern Ireland to keep the fires of conflict burning. I hope and pray that I live to see the day when the Peace Line goes the way of the Berlin Wall: its destruction will be the symbolic end of an age of conflict.

On my first day in Belfast I met with two groups of local officials, businessmen and -women, and the leaders of community and development organizations. One group was nationalist, on their side of the Peace Line. The other was unionist, on their side. I was told that the groups had little or no contact or communication with each other. Yet, to my surprise, they both conveyed essentially the same message. With charts, graphs, and slides, in persuasive presentations, they told me that in Belfast there is a high correlation between unemployment and violence; that unless jobs become available to the young men of the inner city, there cannot be a durable peace. As I sat and listened, I thought I could just as well be in New York, Detroit, Johannesburg, Manila, or any other big city in the world.

The aspirations of people the world over are the same. To satisfy those aspirations they need work. Jobs. Good jobs. Good-paying jobs. Fathers and mothers must be able to satisfy the economic needs of their families: housing, food, health care, education, recreation. They also have to be able to satisfy their own emotional need for productive work, for self-respect, for meaning in their lives.

The dispute in Northern Ireland is not purely or even primarily economic in origin or nature. There are many other strands to this complex conflict. It is, of course, in part religious. It is also very much about national identity: Protestants overwhelmingly want Northern Ireland to remain part of the United Kingdom, in union with England, Scotland, and Wales; thus they are called unionists. Catholics generally want Northern Ireland to become part of a united Ireland; they are called nationalists. But economic deprivation is a contributing factor in the problems in Northern Ireland. Along the Falls Road in Belfast, where the working-class Catholic families congregate, and the Shankill Road, where their Protestant counterparts live, some estimates suggest that as many as a third of the men are born, live out their lives, and die without ever having held a job. For some of these men, I was told, membership in a paramilitary organization offers steady pay and a status that they cannot otherwise achieve. For others, patriotism or idealism or revenge may be sufficient motivation. It is possible, of course, that some are driven by all of these factors and others as well.

On this first trip I gained a sense of the importance attached to American involvement in Northern Ireland. Although my role was minor, there was extensive media coverage of every meeting; my discussions with the community groups were carried live on the radio. I met for the first time many of the men I would come to know well in the coming years: the political leaders of Northern Ireland. I was impressed by their involvement in economic issues, by their candor, and by the extent of their mistrust of "the other side." Most of them were blunt in their negative assessments of the other politicians in Northern Ireland. I didn't know at the time how mild these comments were in comparison to what I would hear later in the negotiations.

I spent nearly a week in Northern Ireland. I was favorably impressed by the energy and intelligence of the people. As I was later to confirm in much more detail, Northern Ireland is an advanced, modern society. Its people are productive, literate, articulate. But for all its modernity and literacy, Northern Ireland has been divided, by a deep and ancient hatred, into two hostile communities, their enmity burnished by centuries of conflict. They have often inflicted hurt, physical and psychological, on members of the other community, and they have been quick to take offense at real or perceived slights. They have a highly developed sense of grievance. As one of the participants in the talks later said to me: "To understand us, Senator, you must realize that we in Northern Ireland will drive 100 miles out of our way to receive an insult." Each is a minority: Catholics in Northern Ireland, Protestants on the island of Ireland. Each sees itself as a victim community, constantly under siege, the recipient of a long litany of violent blows from the other.

As I flew back to the U.S., I thought about how the harsher side of the Northern Irish personality had so dominated the recent past. For a quarter century, violence, and the threat of violence, hung over Northern Ireland like a heavy, unyielding fog. Thousands of people were killed, tens of thousands injured. Fear and anxiety were as much a part of daily life as work and school. But the real damage being done was to people's hearts and minds, where, with each new atrocity, the hostility grew more and more intense. A bombed-out building can be quickly rebuilt, a burned-out car replaced. But as one generation, then another, grew into adulthood knowing so much hate and fear, the prospects for reconciliation receded.

The events of recent years can be understood only in the context of the long history of British domination of Ireland. In the early seventeenth century, at about the time the British began the colonization of North America, they undertook the settlement of Ireland; it was called "the plantation." The policy encouraged settlers from England and Scotland to go to Ireland, the lure being grants of land. As in North America, the settlers landed on the east coast and gradually advanced westward, pushing the native inhabitants ahead of them.

The native Irish were needed to work the land, so their movement to the west was not as complete as in America. Nonetheless, to this day, the western part of Northern Ireland is largely Catholic, the eastern part largely Protestant. Belfast, in the middle of the Protestant heartland, is the capital. The second biggest city is Londonderry (called Derry by Catholics); it is in the west and has a

Catholic majority. In 1922, after centuries of British rule and years of bitter conflict, Ireland obtained its independence. But as a result the island of Ireland was partitioned. The twenty-six counties of the south and west, largely Catholic, became the Irish Free State, and eventually the modern Republic of Ireland. The six counties of the north, with a Protestant majority, remained part of the union.

The government of the newly created Northern Ireland established itself, in the later, memorable words of a unionist leader, as "a Protestant Parliament for a Protestant people." Discrimination against Catholics was widespread. In Londonderry, although Protestants comprised less than half of the population, they controlled the local government through gerrymandering, and they used that power to maintain their dominance.

So it was not surprising that the Catholic civil rights movement found its voice in Londonderry, in the 1960s and 1970s, in the person of John Hume. Young, articulate, a natural leader, he grew up resenting the injustices he felt were being suffered by Catholics. But he could not support the response of those nationalists who support or condone the use of force to expel the British from Northern Ireland.[1] He advocated peaceful protest. He didn't want to throw the unionists out; he wanted to live with them—as equals. Over time, his Social Democratic and Labour Party (SDLP) became the largest nationalist party, and he emerged as the dominant nationalist political leader, gaining election to the European Parliament in 1979 and to the British Parliament in 1983. As the civil rights movement spread across Northern Ireland, violence flared. The inability of the Northern Ireland government to deal with the crisis led to its dissolution in 1972. The British government took direct control of the province, administering its affairs through a Northern Ireland Office.

In the early 1980s, in a series of speeches and articles, Hume argued that the problems of Northern Ireland could not be solved in isolation. He advocated broadly based negotiations to consider simultaneously three relationships: unionists and nationalists within Northern Ireland; the Republic of Ireland and Northern Ireland; and Britain and the Republic of Ireland. Despite the efforts of some of their leaders, relations between the governments of Britain and Ireland had been poor for a long time after the partition of Ireland. It gradually became evident that if there was to be an end to the periodic outbreaks of violence in Northern Ireland, there had to be cooperation between Britain and the Republic.

The politics of modern Ireland derive from the conflict of the early part of this century. Disagreement over the treaty with Britain[2] led to a brief but bitter civil war in the new Irish Free State. The pro-treaty forces, led by Michael Collins, prevailed, and eventually became the modern Fine Gael party. The anti-treaty forces, led by Eamon de Valera, constituted the Fianna Fail party. Thus, Fianna Fail has always been regarded by unionists as the more nationalist (or "green") of the two major Irish parties, and therefore the most suspect.

In 1982, in an effort to return home rule to Northern Ireland, the British government proposed the creation of a new assembly in which there would be a limited form of power-sharing. Nationalists opposed the proposal, demanding the full sharing of power. In the campaign leading up to an election in October of that year, Hume and the SDLP called for the creation of a Council for a New Ireland, to include the main political parties in the Republic of Ireland and the SDLP. It was an attempt to forge a consensus among nationalists as an alternative to the assembly proposed by the British. The assembly was created but nationalists never participated, and it was eventually dissolved in 1986.

In 1983 a Fine Gael Taoiseach,[3] Dr. Garrett Fitzgerald, took up the SDLP proposal and established the New Ireland Forum. It brought together the main parties in the Republic with the SDLP to discuss the shape of what was ambitiously called a "New Ireland." Its report in 1984 set out several principles and requirements for a political settlement in Northern Ireland. It included the statement that Irish unity would come about only "with the consent of the people of the North and of the South of Ireland." This was the most flexible position then possible, since the Fianna Fail platform insisted that the only valid unit for self-determination was the whole island. The report set out three possible models for a New Ireland: a unified Irish state; a federal Ireland; or joint British-Irish sovereignty over Northern Ireland. At Hume's insistence, the report also indicated that the members of the Forum were open to other suggestions. The three models were famously dismissed by then British Prime Minister Margaret Thatcher, as "out, out, out." But they were very much in the minds of unionists when the Anglo-Irish Agreement was reached the following year.

That agreement, reached on November 15, 1985, was a turning point in the history of Northern Ireland. Article One acknowledged that there would be no change in the constitutional status of Northern Ireland without the consent of a majority of the people of Northern Ireland. Thereafter, the British government undertook to discharge its responsibilities in Northern Ireland in consultation with the Irish government (but without any loss of sovereignty). A standing Intergovernmental Conference, co-chaired by the Irish minister for foreign affairs and the British secretary of state for Northern Ireland, was established for this purpose, supported by a permanent joint Secretariat of British and Irish officials based at Maryfield, outside Belfast. Dublin was given the right to be consulted about British policy in relation to Northern Ireland, and the two governments committed themselves to making "determined efforts" to resolve any disagreements.

The unionist community was totally opposed to the Anglo-Irish Agreement, primarily because the role given to the Irish government was interpreted as a step in the direction of "joint sovereignty." The agreement's focus on the Northern Ireland aspects of the intergovernmental relationship also unsettled unionists, because it set Northern Ireland apart from the rest of the United Kingdom, appearing to undermine its constitutional status as an integral part of the U.K. A campaign was organized to reject the agreement. Huge rallies were held, and a petition drive was organized. Assembly and District Council business was disrupted by an "Ulster says No" campaign; normal contact with ministers was broken off. All of the unionist members of Parliament resigned their seats, forcing simultaneous by-elections which were viewed as a referendum on the agreement and which delivered a predictably negative overall result. A "day of action" was organized in March 1986 in an attempt to demonstrate the campaign's ability to bring the agreement down by direct action.

The security forces, led by the Royal Ulster Constabulary, were able to contain the day of action and the other disturbances associated with the "Ulster says No" campaign. Ultimately a Joint Unionist Task Force report, "An End to Drift," acknowledged that the only way forward was to negotiate an alternative to the Anglo-Irish Agreement, and unionist leaders approached the British government in August 1987 to initiate discussions to that end. The subsequent "talks about talks" led ultimately to negotiations in 1991 and 1992, which ended without agreement.

In 1988, Hume received a telephone call from a Belfast solicitor. Would he be willing to meet with Sinn Fein officials to talk about some of the issues he had been publicly discussing? It was a risk for Hume. Sinn Fein is a political party with close ties to the Irish Republican Army (IRA), the paramilitary organization committed to the use of force to achieve a united Ireland. The SDLP and Sinn Fein compete for nationalist votes; anything that might strengthen Sinn Fein politically could weaken the SDLP. But Hume agreed. He met Gerry Adams, the leader of Sinn Fein, for the first time, and they began a dialogue which stretched across six years. It was, for part of that time, a complex set of four-way discussions, involving the SDLP, Sinn Fein, and the Irish and British governments.

The acceptance by Dublin of Article One of the Anglo-Irish Agreement was framed in terms which allowed it to be defended as an acceptance of political realities rather than a commitment to a principle. The effect of the article was subsequently challenged in a case taken to the Irish Supreme Court by two leading unionists. The Court's decision confirmed unionists' worst fears by asserting that the achievement of Irish unity was a "constitutional imperative" on every Irish government and that signature of the Anglo-Irish Agreement had not implied any acceptance that Northern Ireland was constitutionally a part of the United Kingdom.

The agreement had been signed by Garrett Fitzgerald, whose government was succeeded in 1987 by one led by Fianna Fail. In 1992, Albert Reynolds became Taoiseach. Reynolds moved Fianna Fail and the government toward accommodation over Northern Ireland. He entered into two parallel dialogues: with the British prime minister, John Major; and with Hume and Adams, as the three men sought to establish a common nationalist position.

On December 15, 1993, Reynolds and Major announced the Downing Street Declaration. It was another significant step toward peace in Northern Ireland. The Declaration arose primarily from the desire of the British and Irish governments to set out the terms on which parties associated with paramilitary organizations in Northern Ireland could enter negotiations. It also sought to tackle one of the major obstacles to agreement in the 1991–92 talks: the difference of view between the two governments over the constitutional status of Northern Ireland. The Declaration reiterated or expressed a number of key principles which the two governments hoped would provide "the starting point of a peace process designed to culminate in a political settlement." On the main constitutional issue the Declaration provided a resolution of the two governments' conflicting views by upholding the "constitutional guarantee" to unionists that Northern Ireland would not cease to be a part of the United Kingdom without the consent of a majority of its people, while presenting that as part of a new doctrine of Irish national self-determination in which the consent of both parts of Ireland, freely and concurrently given, would be required to bring about Irish unity.

For its part, the British government reiterated that its policy regarding the future constitutional status was based on upholding the democratic wish of the people of Northern Ireland, and that it had "no selfish strategic or economic interest in Northern Ireland," a phrase originally used by the British secretary of state for Northern Ireland, Peter Brooke, in November 1991. It went on to acknowledge that "it is for the people of the island of Ireland alone, by agreement between the two parts respectively, to exercise their right of self-determination on the basis of consent, freely and concurrently given, North and South, to bring about a united Ireland, if that is their wish," and undertook to introduce legislation to give effect to this or any other measure of agreement on future relationships which might be reached.

The Irish government formally acknowledged that "it would be wrong to attempt to impose a united Ireland, in the absence of the freely given consent of a majority of the people of Northern Ireland," and accepted that "the democratic right of self-determination by the people of Ireland as a whole must be achieved and exercised with and subject to the agreement and consent of a majority of the people of Northern Ireland. . . ." The Taoiseach also said that "in the event of an overall settlement the Irish government will, as part of a balanced constitutional accommodation, put forward and support proposals for change in the Irish Constitution which would fully reflect the principle of consent in Northern Ireland." On the participation of parties associated with paramilitary organizations, the governments said that in the circumstances of

> a permanent end to the use of, or support for, paramilitary violence . . . democratically mandated parties which establish a commitment to exclusively peaceful methods and which have shown they abide by the democratic process are free to participate fully in democratic politics and to join in dialogue in due course between the governments and the political parties on the way ahead.

Hume now argued that the Downing Street Declaration removed the basis for the use of force by the republican movement. Their "military campaign" was based on the conviction that the British government was the enemy—that it had selfish strategic interests in Northern Ireland which it would fight to maintain, and that only "physical force" could evict it and create a united Ireland. But, Hume argued, now that London said that it had no such interests in Northern Ireland, that its people could decide their own future, then the rationale for the campaign of violence no longer existed.

British-Irish cooperation was accompanied by a growing war-weariness in Northern Ireland. Families began to long for a more normal life, one not dominated by fear and hatred. The governments and the politicians responded. In 1991 and 1992 negotiations had taken place involving the governments and the four constitutional political parties.[4] Those negotiations failed, in part, the governments believed, because they did not include the political parties associated with the paramilitary organizations; as a result, the negotiations were not accompanied by a cessation of violence. But the Downing Street Declaration had addressed that issue, and those who favored dialogue persisted. By the summer of 1994 anticipation was high. On August 30, the IRA declared "a complete cessation of all military activity." On October 6, the Combined Loyalist Military Command (CLMC), the umbrella group for the Protestant paramilitary counterparts to the IRA, declared a cease-fire.

The effect was immediate. Like spring flowers blooming suddenly, hope and optimism surged, displacing the despair and pessimism that had seemed permanent. The Christmas season of 1994 was the brightest and busiest Belfast had seen in decades. The borders were flung open, and people moved freely between north and south, creating commerce and goodwill. By February 1995, when I arrived, hopes were high. But it was a hope tinged with fear and fatalism. Northern Ireland had been through earlier peace efforts, in 1974 and again in 1991–92, and each time there had been the failure, the letdown, the continuation of sectarian conflict.

Later, when I became well known in Northern Ireland, I was often stopped by strangers, on the street, in the airport, in restaurants. They almost always offered words of gratitude and encouragement: "Thank you, Senator." "God bless you." "We appreciate what you're doing." And then, always, the fear: "But you're wasting your time. We've been killing each other for centuries and we're doomed to go on killing each other forever."

This uneasy mixture of hope and fear was tangible in February 1995. I hoped that somehow the conference on trade and investment could be of benefit. I'll probably never be back, I thought, but it would be nice to be of help. The conference was a success. Hundreds of American businessmen and businesswomen attended, as did a large contingent from Northern Ireland. Most of Northern Ireland's political leaders attended as well. I had to struggle to keep the focus on business and not let it become a political convention. The participants were invited to the White House for a reception in a tent on the south lawn. Despite a driving rain, it went well. Spirits were high as men and women who were bitter opponents gathered in one room and heard urgent pleas for peace, from me, from Secretary of Commerce Ron Brown, and from President Clinton.

The day before the conference began, the president told me he was looking forward to coming to the event, and we reviewed his proposed remarks. In them he would make a number of announcements. Then he said, "There's one more announcement I'd like to make. Everyone would like you to stay on. I know you were originally told it would just be for six months. But we want this thing to have staying power. We want you to help with a trade mission and some other follow-up this fall. I'd like to say tomorrow that you've agreed to stay on until the end of the year."

I didn't hesitate. "I really like the people I've met, and I want to help them if I can. Yes, you can announce it."

CHAPTER 3

First Steps

FOLLOWING up on the trade and investment conference, I traveled to the United Kingdom for two weeks in late June and early July, dividing my time between London and Northern Ireland. On this trip I met more political and business leaders and started to get a better sense of the complexity of the conflict. I began an intensive study of its origins, reading several books on the tangled history of relations between Britain and Ireland.

I was in Northern Ireland again in late November and early December 1995. It was a decisive turning point for me. I had been involved with Northern Ireland for nearly a year, but only in a limited way. That was about to change.

My office was in the State Department, and from time to time I briefed Peter Tarnoff, the undersecretary of state, on my activities. Since the Commerce Department implemented the day-to-day aspects of our trade and investment policy in Northern Ireland, I also kept Ron Brown abreast of developments. Brown was interested in Northern Ireland and made sure that his department actively supported the president's policy there.

My principal contacts were at the White House. They were Anthony Lake, the president's national security adviser, and Nancy Soderberg, Tony's assistant, whose area of responsibility included Northern Ireland. They were both friends of long standing. Tony had worked with me on Edmund Muskie's presidential campaign in 1971 and 1972. Nancy had been on Senator Ted Kennedy's staff for several years. They knew a lot about Northern Ireland and they were very helpful to me. More than any other person, Nancy had initially formulated and shaped my role in Northern Ireland.

Tony was, of course, aware of the president's keen personal interest, and was, on his own, just as interested. He followed the matter closely; he regularly met, and spoke often by telephone, with a wide range of British and Irish government officials and political leaders in Northern Ireland. Tony served the president well, giving him regular briefings and sound policy advice.

In November, Tony told me that the British and Irish governments were thinking about creating an international commission to make recommendations on the difficult issue of the disarmament of paramilitary organizations. The effort by the governments to get negotiations started had stalled over the issue.

On the nationalist side, the major paramilitary organization is the IRA. Its "political wing" is Sinn Fein. There are several unionist paramilitary organizations, four of them associated with political parties: the Red Hand Commandos and the Ulster Volunteer Force (UVF) are connected to the Progressive Unionist Party (PUP); the Ulster Defense Association (UDA) and the Ulster Freedom Fighters (UFF) are associated with the Ulster Democratic Party (UDP). The PUP and the UDP are known collectively as "loyalist" parties. The four Protestant paramilitary organizations cooperated for a time under the Combined Loyalist Military Command (CLMC).

Later, during the course of discussions between the International Body on Decommissioning of weapons and representatives of Sinn Fein, I asked Gerry Adams whether he spoke for the IRA. He said no. When I asked officials of the loyalist parties if they spoke for the paramilitary organizations to which they were linked they said yes.

Sinn Fein has consistently denied any relationship with the IRA. That denial is believed by few in Ireland, north and south, or in Britain. The police and security services of both the British and Irish governments told us that they had overwhelming evidence of a close relationship between Sinn Fein and the IRA, including overlapping leadership. The IRA is illegal in the United Kingdom and the Republic of Ireland. Membership in the organization, if proven, is punishable by imprisonment. When the IRA declared a cease-fire in August 1994, it said that:

Recognizing the potential of the current situation and in order to enhance the democratic peace process and to underline our definitive commitment to its success, the leadership [of the IRA] have decided that from midnight there will be a complete cessation of military operations. All our units have been instructed accordingly.

On October 6 the major unionist paramilitary organizations announced their cease-fire through the Combined Loyalist Military Command:

> After a widespread consultative process initiated by representations from the Ulster Democratic and Progressive Unionist Parties, and after having received confirmation and guarantees in relation to Northern Ireland's constitutional position with the United Kingdom, as well as other assurances, and, in the belief that the democratically expressed wishes of the greater number of people in Northern Ireland will be respected and upheld, the C.L.M.C. will universally cease all operational hostilities as from 12 midnight on Thursday the 13th October 1994.

Republicans claimed that the IRA declared its cease-fire in the expectation, based on assurances from the British government, that inclusive political negotiations would begin immediately. But unionist leaders were mistrustful and wary; before entering into any negotiations they demanded assurances that the cease-fire was "permanent." The British government took the same position, and a lengthy public debate followed on the precise meaning of the words used by the IRA in its cease-fire declaration, particularly the absence of the word "permanent." London denied that it had given the IRA any assurances about inclusive political negotiations.

Over the winter of 1994–95, the debate grew louder and more confusing. There was criticism by some nationalists in the Republic and in Northern Ireland over what was seen as the British government's squandering the opportunity presented by the cease-fires. So London decided to clarify and explain its policy.

On March 7, 1995, the British secretary of state for Northern Ireland, Sir Patrick Mayhew, addressed a gathering in Washington organized by U.S. Secretary of State Warren Christopher. Mayhew emphasized the need "to begin the process of decommissioning arms, both IRA and Loyalist," and he summed up the British position in his concluding remarks:

So we shall be pressing to achieve three things:

- A willingness in principle to disarm progressively;
- A common practical understanding of the modalities, that is to say, what decommissioning would actually entail;
- In order to test the practical arrangements and to demonstrate good faith, the actual decommissioning of some arms as a tangible confidence building measure and to signal the start of a process.

That is how Sinn Fein can remove their self-imposed disqualification, and take their place at the talks table where a lasting settlement can be negotiated upon equal terms.

Unfortunately, what was intended as a way out of the impasse solidified it instead. The third provision—that there had to be "actual decommissioning of some arms" "to demonstrate good faith"—became known as Washington Three: the demand for some disarmament before inclusive negotiations could begin.

As 1995 wore on, Washington Three increasingly became the focus of discussion and the basis of the stalemate. As the debate continued, the rhetoric on both sides became more heated and their positions hardened. At the invitation of the British and Irish governments, President Clinton planned a visit to those countries, including a day in Northern Ireland. As plans for the president's trip moved forward, the peace process seemed to be moving backward.

The Irish government had long sought to involve outsiders, to "internationalize" the problem of Northern Ireland. The Irish especially wanted to get the Americans involved. The British had resisted, on the grounds that Northern Ireland was part of the United Kingdom so the conflict there was an internal issue; to internationalize it could undermine British sovereignty. Now, Tony Lake told me, the British government, although still reluctant, was prepared to join the Irish government in creating an international group to study and make recommendations on the thorny issue of disarmament. They were even prepared to accept an American as chairman of the group: me.

As Tony described it, the British were influenced by three factors: they wanted to accommodate the Irish government, which was pressing very hard for direct American involvement; they did not want to offend or embarrass President Clinton; and they had been reassured by my performance as special advisor to the president. They were hopeful that I would be, and be seen as, fair and impartial, and thus be acceptable to both communities in the north. Besides, my presence would be balanced by that of two non-Americans: a Canadian chosen by the British, and a Finn picked by the Irish. I was later told by both London and Dublin officials that the British were most worried about offending President Clinton as he visited London, Belfast, and Dublin. They consented to the international commission with grave reservations and only at the last minute. Both governments wanted prompt action, so Tony assured me that it would take only a couple of months. It sounded like an interesting and challenging assignment that wouldn't take long, and I readily accepted. A short while later, I received formal, confirming calls from both governments. The president's trip took on new meaning for me.

It was a successful visit by any standard. The president and Hillary Rodham Clinton were warmly received in London, cheered in Belfast, and embraced in Dublin. Huge crowds greeted them with a rousing enthusiasm. The president rose to the occasion. His speeches were concise and to the point, reassuring to both sides; his informal remarks were eloquent. He was the first American president to visit Northern Ireland while in office, the first to make ending the conflict there a high priority for the U.S. government. His interest in and knowledge of the subject came through, and the people voiced their appreciation.

I attended some events with the president but spent most of my time on the trip getting organized for my next task. I made contact by telephone with my new colleagues. John de Chastelain was about to retire as chief of the Canadian Defense Forces. He had served two separate terms in the position, an unusual distinction. In between, he served for a year as the Canadian ambassador to the United States. I had met him then. Although I didn't know him well, I had a favorable impression, which was later confirmed. He is intelligent, disciplined, and precise—just what you would want and expect in a top military man.

Harri Holkeri, chosen by the Irish, served as prime minister of Finland from 1987 to 1991, capping a successful twenty-year career in public service. When we met for the first time, in New York in early December, I encountered a tall, ruggedly handsome man in his late fifties. Physically fit—he ran the New York marathon at the age of forty-five—and mentally sharp, he displayed throughout our relationship strong leadership and sound judgment.

The three of us worked together for two and a half years, as members of what came to be known as the International Body on Decommissioning of weapons, and then as the independent chairmen of the peace talks. We never had a serious disagreement, substantive or personal. My two colleagues and their staffs were a pleasure to work with: fair, open-minded, willing to work hard. De Chastelain and Holkeri deserve a lot more credit than they have received for their efforts.

Among the meetings I attended with the president were those he had with Ian Paisley, Gerry Adams, and David Trimble. Adams, a Catholic, the president of Sinn Fein, is deeply committed to a united Ireland. Paisley, leader of the Democratic Unionist Party (DUP), and Trimble, the head of the Ulster Unionist Party (UUP), are Protestants and are just as deeply committed to the continued union of Northern Ireland with the United Kingdom. Although Paisley and Trimble are in agreement on the union, they disagree on how best to achieve that objective and they compete vigorously for unionist votes. Different as they were in background, religion, politics, and temperament, all three had in common the skills necessary for survival in the dangerous swirl of politics in Northern Ireland: intelligence, political savvy, a well-honed sense of their communities, the ability to rouse a crowd through powerful oratory, an understanding of the importance of an occasional act of flamboyance (in Paisley's case more than occasional), and an unerring mastery of the TV sound bite.

Adams and Paisley also shared an approach to the president of the United States. Clinton's meetings with these two key leaders took place back to back, late at night, after the president had had a long, grueling day. Admiral Bill Crowe, then the U.S. ambassador to the United Kingdom, and I were also present. (I had met Adams before, in my position as special advisor to the president. Paisley had refused to see me, so this was my first meeting with him. It was not the last. I would later spend many long hours listening to his unique brand of oratory.) First Paisley and then Adams came in, each with a couple of aides. Twenty minutes had been set aside for each meeting. Each lasted about thirty minutes.

President Clinton was dead tired, his face drawn, his voice hoarse. Fortunately for him, he didn't have to say anything other than "Hello" and "Good-bye." Paisley immediately launched into a thirty-minute recitation of the history of Northern Ireland from the unionist point of view. It was a fascinating story, well told, totally one-sided, and yet persuasive if the listener knew nothing else about Northern Ireland. There was virtually no discussion, and it was all very polite. Paisley and his group left, and a few minutes later Adams came in with his entourage.

Almost exactly the same thing happened. Adams delivered the history of Northern Ireland from the nationalist point of view. It too was a fascinating story, well told, also persuasive. Adams was not as emotional and expressive as Paisley had been, but he was every bit as articulate. Again, it was polite, but there was no discussion.

We left for the Europa Hotel for the meeting with Trimble. Because it was so late, and because the president was so obviously exhausted, it was a short, cordial session. Later as I lay in bed trying to sleep, I wondered how it was possible to have two such completely different views of the same society. I thought that part of the answer must lie in the segregation of the society. Although they are important political leaders in a small society (there are about one and a half million people in Northern Ireland), Adams and Paisley had never met or spoken to each other. Other than in large assemblies, they still haven't, and I doubt they ever will.

Holkeri, de Chastelain, and I, and our staffs, met in New York on December 9 to get organized. I was impressed by their appetite for work. I wanted to get started right away, to consult with as many people with as many different points of view as possible. That would be difficult in the limited time the governments had given us—they wanted our report in January. With Christmas intervening, we had only a few weeks. I was pleased to learn that my colleagues were as anxious as I was to get going.

With a brief break for Christmas, we spent the next six weeks shuttling between Belfast, London, and Dublin. We met with dozens of government officials, political leaders, and business and religious leaders. With the exception of Paisley, who refused to meet with us, we saw almost every major political figure. We heard Paisley's views by talking at length with some of his close political allies. We worked long hours every day, listening, asking questions, taking notes. Then we retreated to the Churchill Hotel in London for several days to make our decisions and write our report. There we reviewed our notes and our recollections and the positions of the parties.

The positions on decommissioning were clear. The British government and some of the unionist parties—the UUP, the DUP, and the United Kingdom Unionist Party (UKUP) led by Robert McCartney, a close ally of Paisley—were on one side. They insisted that the paramilitary organizations would have to give up their arms before the political parties with which they were associated could enter any negotiations. The political parties linked to the paramilitary organizations on both sides insisted that there could be no disarmament until after the negotiations were completed and an agreement reached. The Irish government and the largest nationalist party, the Social Democratic and Labour Party (SDLP), were somewhere in the middle: they wanted disarmament but feared that making it a precondition to negotiations would mean that there would never be negotiations. That point of view was repeated to us many times during our consultations. It wasn't just the Irish government and the SDLP who insisted that there would never be decommissioning prior to negotiations. Other parties, north and south, religious leaders, business leaders, and community activists, nationalist and unionist, repeated the argument. The British government had gotten itself on the hook of prior decommissioning, we were told, and we had been brought in to get them off.

The clinching argument came from the top British police officer in Northern Ireland. The police force there is known as the Royal Ulster Constabulary (RUC). At its head is the chief constable, at that time Hugh Annesley. We went to the RUC headquarters, where we met with Annesley and his principal assistants, who were friendly, informative, and candid. Annesley is an intelligent, thoughtful man. When I asked him whether, if Gerry Adams wanted to, he could persuade the IRA to decommission prior to negotiations, Annesley replied, flatly, "No, he couldn't do it even if he wanted to. He doesn't have that much control over them." All his top officials agreed. In a later meeting, Irish police and security officials expressed the same opinion in even stronger terms. That seemed to us to make the case against prior decommissioning convincing.

We continued to meet on a regular basis with ministers and civil servants from both governments. When we told some of the British officials what we were hearing in our consultations, and particularly what we had heard from the RUC, they expressed concern. To our surprise (because we knew of no reason for it), they appeared to believe that we were simply going to reaffirm their position on prior decommissioning. Now, concerned that we might recommend something else, they asked us to go to London to meet with Prime Minister John Major. In fact, we were thinking of recommending "parallel decommissioning." One side was taking the position that there had to be decommissioning *before* negotiations could begin. The other was arguing that there could be no decommissioning until *after* negotiations ended. The obvious compromise was to recommend that negotiations and decommissioning occur in parallel. This had been tried, successfully, in El Salvador just a few years earlier. I had spoken with some officials at the United Nations who had been involved in El Salvador, and reviewed some of their documents. The circumstances were different, but the principle seemed applicable.

A few days later we entered the Cabinet Room at 10 Downing Street. There, arrayed across the table, were the British government's top officials on Northern Ireland: Prime Minister Major;

Secretary of State for Northern Ireland Mayhew; Minister for Northern Ireland Michael Ancram; the prime minister's personal assistant; and a host of others.

Major is of average height, slender and graying. On this day, as always when I met him, he wore a pink shirt and a dark suit. With his large, horn-rimmed glasses, he looked like the banker he once was. He is friendly and charming, but tough enough to have reached the top in the rough-and-tumble of British politics. He was not able to keep his fractious party together in the 1997 election (it is doubtful that anyone could have), and it went down to a crushing defeat. But in early 1996, as we took our seats in the elegant, high-ceilinged room where so much history had been made, I knew that Major was trying hard, in difficult political circumstances, to keep the peace process in Northern Ireland alive. For that, I admired him. On a personal level I liked his warmth and candor. I was also keenly aware that he had created the International Body on Decommissioning, with an American chairman, overriding critics in his own party. The last thing in the world I wanted to do was to embarrass him.

He was polite, as always. He asked how things were going, and whether we had made any decisions on our report. I told him that we had made no decisions. I then reported on what we had been told, particularly by the RUC; they were, after all, his government's officials. A lively discussion followed. Prior to the meeting Major's aides had obtained from Annesley a letter that modified and explained his statements to us but which did not alter his conclusion. I felt sorry for Annesley. He had been truthful with us, and now, because his opinion didn't fit with the government's policy, it became obvious that his honesty with us had gotten him in trouble with his superiors.

Finally, Major spoke directly to us. His words had a steely candor. If we recommended parallel decommissioning he would have to reject the report. He didn't want to, but he would have to. In reply, I acknowledged that when the governments asked us to serve on the International Body, they had made it clear that they were not bound in advance to accept our recommendations. That seemed to me to be a reasonable precaution on their parts. So he could reject our report. He had to do what he thought was right. We respected that. At the same time, we knew he would understand that we had to do what we thought right. We hoped he would respect that. I asked de Chastelain and Holkeri if they wanted to add anything. They simply said they agreed with me. I was grateful for this; we had not anticipated Major's bluntness, so we had not worked out an agreed response in advance. Much later, after we had worked together for years, we could read each other's expressions and thoughts. But at this time, we had known each other for barely a month.

After we left 10 Downing Street, we met privately. We took Major's words seriously, but they did not change our minds. We had been told by many people that the British government expected us to recommend a change in their policy on prior decommissioning. But Major had given no hint of such an expectation. He had strongly defended his policy.

We were convinced that the prior decommissioning policy was unworkable. The British wanted inclusive negotiations, and they wanted prior decommissioning—but clearly they could not have both. How could we help them see that? More importantly, what could we recommend in place of prior decommissioning that would provide the unionists with enough reassurance to enable them to enter into negotiations?

The unionists' fears were real and well founded. For years the republican movement had pursued a dual strategy described as the armalite and the ballot box: Use the political process to make what gains were possible, and at the same time maintain the use, and the threat, of violence to move the political process along. Indeed, it was an article of faith among some republicans that the British government would change its Northern Ireland policy only as a reaction to violence, especially in Britain. The unionist nightmare was that they would be forced to enter talks with Sinn Fein while a heavily armed IRA waited outside the door; at the first sign that Sinn Fein wasn't getting what it wanted in the talks the campaign of violence would resume.

There were, of course, strong counterarguments. Since any weapons handed in could be quickly replaced, prior decommissioning was a political policy and was not related to genuine security needs. In the end, the attitudes of the participants would matter most, and if discussions never got underway, how would anyone know whether the desire for peace and negotiation was genuine?

Our response was to formulate a set of principles to which any party wanting to enter negotiations would have to commit itself. We called them principles of democracy and nonviolence, and they eventually became known as the Mitchell Principles. We worked on them for several days, testing them for logic and practicality. They had to be strong and meaningful enough to attract the unionists, while not so impractical as to turn off the other political parties. We considered including the concept of parallel decommissioning as one of the principles, but we hadn't yet thought and talked it through carefully enough to reach a final decision. Then Michael Ancram, the British minister in Northern Ireland, called with an invitation to dinner. We were happy to accommodate him. We met at the Dunadry Inn, a few miles outside of Belfast.

Ancram worked directly under, and reported to, Sir Patrick Mayhew. Ancram is stocky, with curly black hair and an informal manner that masks his aristocratic background. He is calm, intelligent, and unusually resourceful. Later, when the negotiations got underway, he was repeatedly attacked by Paisley, McCartney, and their allies, often in the most personally insulting terms. Ancram never lost his cool; he responded when necessary, often with wit, and shrugged off the criticism when the best reply was silence. No matter how difficult the situation, he could always find some reason for hope and optimism.

Now, as we chatted easily over dinner, I knew he was there for a purpose, and I wondered what he would suggest. He stressed the importance of an election from which delegates to the negotiations would be drawn. When the two governments announced the creation of the International Body on Decommissioning in November, they had accompanied it with a second "track," under which they committed themselves to begin inclusive negotiations. The unionists insisted that any negotiations had to be preceded by an election; to accommodate them, the British wanted us to include a reference to an election in our report. Then, late in the evening, Ancram asked softly, "If you're going to suggest parallel decommissioning, have you thought about putting it in a separate section of your report, not as a recommendation but simply as a suggestion for the governments to consider?"

To keep our options open I said we hadn't made a decision yet, but that we would give his suggestion some thought. But what I thought was, Of course. Parallel decommissioning doesn't fit in with the principles of democracy and nonviolence. It's not a principle. It's a pragmatic compromise to a difficult political problem.

After our initial meeting at 10 Downing Street, Ancram had become convinced we were not going to support the British policy on prior decommissioning, and he wanted to soften the impact of parallel decommissioning. He provided the final piece to our puzzle. We were later to spend several long days and nights at the Churchill Hotel putting the pieces together and honing the language, but when my two colleagues and I conferred briefly after our dinner with Ancram, the outline of our report was clear in my mind.

I woke up the next morning thinking about Bob McCartney. Earlier, during the process of consultation, we had met with the leadership of the UKUP. McCartney dominated the party and the discussion. He is an interesting star in the constellation of Northern Ireland politics. Tall, silver-haired, articulate, with a deep and resonating voice, he is one of Northern Ireland's most successful barristers. He was born into a poor Protestant family in Belfast and rose to success through talent and hard work. He entered politics as a moderate unionist who seemed to offer an alternative to the negativism of Ian Paisley. Early in his career he publicly called Paisley a fascist. But he won election to the Parliament as an independent only because Paisley's party, the DUP, did not field a candidate against him; had they done so, many believed, McCartney could not have won. I don't know whether it was for that reason or on the basis of conviction, but by the time I got to Northern Ireland McCartney had become a close ally of Paisley.

At the very beginning of our meeting, McCartney bluntly challenged us: Would we be truly independent, or would we let the British government write our report? I assured him that, although we would openly seek the advice of the governments, as we were now seeking his, and although we would take good ideas wherever we found them, in the end the report would be ours.

I have always found it useful to subject my actions to analysis by those who disagree with me. Since McCartney was skeptical about our relationship with the British government, I tried to look at our recent actions from his perspective. Had he been a silent witness to our meeting with the prime minister, and then to our dinner with Ancram, would he have concluded that we were being dictated to, and thereby lacking in independence? Or would he have believed that by rejecting outright the British position on prior decommissioning we were demonstrating our independence?

It was impossible to know, but the more I thought about it, the more secure I felt with our decision. In the real world of Northern Ireland, prior decommissioning simply was not a practical solution. That was so clear that I wondered whether someone as astute as John Major ever really believed that we would simply endorse it. But it was equally impractical to think that the unionists would enter into negotiations with nothing to reassure them on the critical issue of paramilitary arms.

Finally, we rejected prior decommissioning. We offered instead an alternative that included three elements: (1) we required that to be eligible to participate in negotiations a party would have to promise to adhere to specific principles of democracy and nonviolence; (2) we suggested that the parties consider parallel decommissioning; and (3) we set forth a detailed process to achieve decommissioning.

The principles of democracy and nonviolence were comprehensive, and they directly addressed the unionists' concerns. We explained and set them forth in these words:

> To reach an agreed political settlement and to take the gun out of Irish politics, there must be commitment and adherence to fundamental principles of democracy and non-violence. Participants in all-party negotiations should affirm their commitment to such principles.
>
> Accordingly, we recommend that the parties to such negotiations affirm their total and absolute commitment:
>
> a. To democratic and exclusively peaceful means of resolving political issues;
> b. To the total disarmament of all paramilitary organizations;
> c. To agree that such disarmament must be verifiable to the satisfaction of an independent commission;

d. To renounce for themselves, and to oppose any effort by others, to use force, or threaten to use force, to influence the course or the outcome of all-party negotiations;

e. To agree to abide by the terms of any agreement reached in all-party negotiations and to resort to democratic and exclusively peaceful methods in trying to alter any aspect of that outcome with which they may disagree; and,

f. To urge that "punishment" killings and beatings stop and to take effective steps to prevent such actions.

In a separate section of the report, we suggested that the parties consider parallel decommissioning.

The parties should consider an approach under which some decommissioning would take place during the process of all-party negotiations, rather than before or after as the parties now urge. Such an approach represents a compromise. If the peace process is to move forward, the current impasse must be overcome. While both sides have been adamant in their positions, both have repeatedly expressed the desire to move forward. This approach provides them that opportunity.

We believed this to be a reasonable compromise between two diametrically opposed and strongly held views. We also felt it was practical, in the sense that it wasn't just a theoretical exercise in the art of compromise, but a down-to-earth alternative that could help to get negotiations started.

We were attempting at the same time to confront another problem that didn't seem to us as significant but in the end had profound consequences. The governments' mandate to us was narrowly focused on the controversy over paramilitary arms. But the advice we received during our consultations ranged far beyond that issue, covering many of the problems in Northern Ireland. There were allegations of inequality in employment and housing, and the use of plastic bullets by the RUC. There were disagreements about language, flags, anthems, and national symbols. Indeed, for some of those with whom we met, decommissioning wasn't an issue but rather a red herring that had been used to prevent negotiations from taking place.

How should we deal with these and other issues that were clearly important, but, in a legal sense, outside of our mandate? We could ignore them and produce a narrow, tightly focused report. Or we could cover them all and produce a long, wide-ranging report. Perhaps inevitably, we chose a middle ground.

At the heart of all of the problems in Northern Ireland is mistrust. Centuries of conflict have generated hatreds that make it virtually impossible for the two communities to trust each other. Each disbelieves the other. Each assumes the worst about the other. If there is ever to be durable peace and genuine reconciliation, what is really needed is the decommissioning of mind-sets in Northern Ireland. That means that trust and confidence must be built, over time, by actions in all parts of society. We reasoned that it was appropriate to include in our report our belief in the general need for confidence-building measures and to refer specifically to those which had been called to our attention during our consultations.

During the month of January, as we consulted and deliberated, the question of an election prior to negotiations erupted into a highly publicized controversy. The Ulster Unionists proposed it and David Trimble became its champion. The nationalists opposed it and John Hume became its primary critic. Trimble argued that on a matter so crucial to the future of Northern Ireland, the people should have a say in who the negotiators were going to be.

Hume felt that it was just another unionist delaying tactic; the IRA had been on cease-fire for about a year and a half and still there were no negotiations. How long would the cease-fire hold? Besides, Hume argued, an election campaign would inevitably generate harsh, sectarian rhetoric that would make any subsequent negotiations even more difficult.

We received numerous suggestions on language for the election portion of our report on confidence-building measures: by letter, by fax, by telephone, in person. The British government was particularly anxious that we include a reference to an election, since it was an important part of Major's strategy. We weighed them all and decided on a brief, general paragraph:

Several oral and written submissions raised the idea of an elected body. We note the reference in paragraph three of the Communiqué to "whether and how an elected body could play a part." Elections held in accordance with democratic principles express and reflect the popular will. If it were broadly acceptable, with an appropriate mandate, and within the three-strand structure, an elective process could contribute to the building of confidence.

Those few words pleased Trimble and displeased Hume. But as an architect of the peace process, Hume was totally committed to moving forward. As he was to do so often in his long and patient career, even though he disagreed with Major's subsequent decision to hold an election, he accepted it in the interest of the process.

We set Tuesday, January 23, 1996, as the day on which we would make our report public. We felt it fair and appropriate to give the governments an early look at the report, but we did not want to offer them any opportunity to propose changes. So we delivered to them a copy of the final report on that Monday, January 22, and dated it accordingly. That gave them a day to review it and consider what their reactions should be after the public release.

On Sunday evening, there was a comical, last-minute glitch in the production of the report. The computer at the Churchill Hotel developed a bug, and the printed-out copies of what was supposed to be the final version were garbled. We were working on a very tight time schedule; some staff members were to fly to Dublin and Belfast to hand-deliver copies to Irish and British government officials; other copies were to be hand-delivered to the prime minister's office in London. For a while it appeared as though we would not be able to meet our own schedule. But de Chastelain and three members of our staff—Martha Pope, David Angell, and David Pozorski—were able to figure out what was wrong and fix it. The report was retyped, reproduced, and delivered on schedule.

We had anticipated the reactions by Trimble and Hume to the section on elections. What we had not anticipated was John Major's reaction.

CHAPTER 4

A Different Route

GERRY Adams accused John Major of "unilaterally dumping" the International Body's report. It wasn't support, but it wasn't exactly a dumping. It was a temporary sidestep to get to negotiations by a different route.

When Major went before the House of Commons on January 24, he had a political problem. The day before, in a widely publicized press conference, we had released our report. In it we set forth our conclusion that there would not be the prior decommissioning on which London had insisted before negotiations could begin. While the governments were not bound in advance to accept our report, the widely favorable reaction to it made it difficult for Major to reject. He handled the situation with political skill.

He reviewed our report, heaped praise on it, then proceeded to suggest an alternate route to negotiations. In our sixty-two paragraphs, only one dealt with elections, the one suggesting that an election process could contribute to the building of confidence. Major picked up that sentence and worked it into a different way to the negotiations. He told the House:

> The Government believe that such an elective process offers a viable alternative direct to the confidence necessary to bring about all-party negotiations. In this context it is possible to imagine decommissioning and such negotiations being taken forward in parallel.
>
> ... [W]e believe that, in the light of the Mitchell report, there are two ways in which all-party negotiations can now be

taken forward. Both are fully consistent with the six principles set out in the report.

The first is for the paramilitaries to make a start to decommissioning before all-party negotiations. They can if they will. If not, the second is to secure a democratic mandate for all-party negotiations through elections specially for that purpose.

Two routes to all-party negotiations and to decommissioning. The choice between them is ultimately for the parties themselves.

By proposing an alternate route to negotiations, Major signaled his willingness to move away from prior decommissioning. Although he was heavily criticized for his reaction to our report, Major's strategy proved to be workable. By focusing on elections, he provided the reassurance that the unionists needed, and he deflected attention away from his eventual abandonment of prior decommissioning.

The Irish government received our report warmly, as did many commentators and analysts. Typical was the comment of the *Irish Times*, which said of us: "Their brisk, no-nonsense approach to the matter in hand, the balance and clarity of their analysis, and their role as non-participants in the party game have brought a refreshing new element into the debate."[1]

Holkeri returned to Finland, de Chastelain to Canada, and I came home to the United States. I believed that my work was finished. I had been involved in Ireland for a year. It had been exciting and interesting, and now it was over. My thoughts turned to my wife and my business activities, both of which I had badly ignored for months.

But I couldn't quite let go of Ireland. And it wouldn't let me go. On Saturday, February 3, I taped an interview with David Frost which was broadcast the next morning in London. I warned that the cease-fire that had been in place for a year and a half might soon end. I had no inside information or crystal ball; it just seemed to me to be plain common sense. The IRA had declared a cease-fire in August 1994 in the expectation that inclusive negotiations would begin immediately. Now, eighteen months later, there were no negotiations in sight. The British and Irish governments knew that there were tensions within the IRA leadership over the cease-fire; the vote in favor of it in the IRA Army Council had been close. The British had hotly denied that the IRA had been given assurances of immediate inclusive negotiations. But as the weeks and then months rolled by, with the governments and the parties mired in mostly public exchanges over who said what and who met with whom, it seemed inevitable to me that there would be a return to violence.

On the evening of February 9, a huge explosion rocked London. Two people were killed, a hundred injured, and the property damage was in the millions of pounds. The IRA claimed responsibility. The cease-fire was over.

The bomb went off just before I boarded a plane in Boston bound for Washington. Not knowing what had happened, I stepped off the plane into the glare of television lights and a crowd of reporters. They told me the news and asked for my reaction. I was guarded in my response. I wanted to be sure of the facts before making any detailed comments. I had been burned before, while in the Senate, answering a question based on what I had been told by a reporter, and then learning that his information had been incorrect. I was determined not to let that happen to me in dealing with Northern Ireland.

Once I was fully briefed, I issued a strong statement of condemnation. Whatever the facts about the discussions leading up to the cease-fire, there was no justification for a return to violence. The bombing of cities, the killing and maiming of innocent civilians: these were cowardly acts.

Because of my remarks on the Frost show a few days earlier, I was deluged by requests for comment. Reporters asked over and over again how I had "known" that the IRA was going to end its cease-fire. The more I denied any inside knowledge, the more certain they were that I had such knowledge. They simply wouldn't accept the truth.

On February 28 the British and Irish governments held a "summit" meeting in London. The top officials on Northern Ireland were there: for the British, Prime Minister Major, Secretary of State Mayhew, and the ministers of state, Ancram and Sir John Wheeler; for the Irish, the Taoiseach, John Bruton, was accompanied by the

Deputy Prime Minister and Foreign Minister Dick Spring, and by Minister for Justice Nora Owen.

In a joint communiqué issued after the meeting, the prime ministers announced that inclusive, all-party negotiations on Northern Ireland would be convened on June 10, 1996, following an election process. The details of the election were to be worked out in consultations, which would take place between March 4 and 13, with the Northern Ireland political parties. The prime ministers said that while they wanted Sinn Fein to participate in the negotiations, the party could not do so unless the IRA reinstated its cease-fire. Much of the language of the communiqué was drawn from the report of the International Body, and the prime ministers specifically required that "all participants would need to make clear at the beginning of the discussions their total and absolute commitment to the principles of democracy and non-violence set out in the report of The International Body. They would also need to address, at that stage, its proposals on decommissioning." So while Holkeri, de Chastelain, and I were no longer in the act, our report was at center stage.

The decision by the governments was a huge step forward. But its timing was unfortunate. After a year and a half of seeming inaction, the governments had acted decisively within three weeks of an IRA bomb in London. The governments strongly denied any causal relationship, but the timing made that denial difficult for many republicans and much of the media to accept.

The important thing was that the process was moving. The governments were committed to inclusive negotiations and to a specific date for their commencement. A week later, London and Dublin published consultation papers on the method of election and on the option of an elected forum to run parallel to the negotiations. On March 15, the governments published another consultation paper, this one entitled "Ground Rules for Substantive All-Party Negotiations." It set forth proposed rules under which the negotiations would be conducted.

Following extensive consultation, Major announced his decision on an election in the House of Commons on March 21. He described the three main systems of election proposed by the parties and noted that no consensus on any one of them had emerged among the political parties. So Major made up a new system:

Electors will have to register just one vote which they will cast for the party of their choice. Five seats in each of the eighteen constituencies will be allocated from party constituency lists of candidates, published in advance, in proportion to each party's share of the vote. In addition, the votes in all the constituencies will be aggregated and the ten most successful parties across the whole of Northern Ireland will secure two elected representatives each, from party lists published in advance.

Beneath the legal language was a skillfully constructed political compromise. The unionists wanted an election to an institution, to be called a Forum, where delegates could debate issues, and they got it. The nationalists wanted inclusive negotiations by a date certain, and they got this. The nationalists were opposed to a Forum; but if one was to be created, they didn't want it to have any control over the negotiations. They got that assurance. Each party was to nominate its delegates to the negotiations from among those elected to the Forum, but there was to be no other formal relationship. Both governments wanted the political parties associated with paramilitary organizations to be included in the negotiations. Sinn Fein would clearly get enough votes in any system to be eligible once the IRA reinstated its cease-fire; it was already the fourth largest party in Northern Ireland. But its unionist counterparts, the Progressive Unionist Party and the Ulster Democratic Party—known collectively as the loyalist parties—were new and small, not large enough to win a place at the talks in the election systems customarily used in Northern Ireland. So the British created a new system to get them in, by providing, in a society where there were five well-established parties, that the top *ten* parties would be eligible. The plan was ingenious.

The election to the Forum produced the following results:

Party	Number of Seats in the Forum
Ulster Unionist Party (UUP)	30
Democratic Unionist Party (DUP)	24
Social Democratic and Labour Party (SDLP)	21
Sinn Fein (SF)	17
Alliance (All)	7

United Kingdom Unionist Party (UKUP)	3
Progressive Unionist Party (PUP)	2
Ulster Democratic Party (UDP)	2
Northern Ireland Women's Coalition (NIW)	2
Labour (Lab)	2

The results were interesting in several respects. Although the SDLP received more votes than the DUP (21.37 percent to 18.80 percent), because of the voting system the DUP got more seats in the Forum. The spread between the largest party and the smallest was enormous: the UUP got 24.17 percent of the vote, Labour got 0.85 percent. As expected, the five established parties led the field. The smallest of the five, the Alliance Party, was the only one that tried to attract voters from both communities. With its ability to move across the divide between the two communities, it would play an important role in the negotiations. Alliance was headed by an experienced, articulate team: Lord John Alderdice, a practicing psychologist, was the leader, and Seamus Close the deputy leader. Both were key participants through the two years of negotiations. (Alderdice has since resigned his party position to become speaker-designate of the new Northern Ireland Assembly.)

Among the second tier of five were parties and personalities that would eventually play important roles in the negotiations. The two loyalist parties made it. So did the UKUP, headed by McCartney. Two very small new parties also got in: the Northern Ireland Women's Coalition, headed by Monica McWilliams, a Catholic, and Pearl Sager, a Protestant; and Labour, headed by Malachi Curran and Hugh Casey (this Labour Party is unrelated to the British Labour Party).

The women overcame a great deal of adversity. Early in the process they were not taken seriously in our talks and they were insulted in the Forum. I would not permit such conduct in the negotiations, but it took many months for their courage and commitment to earn the attention and respect of the other parties. In the final stages of the negotiations they were serious, important participants, and were treated as such.

As intended, the Forum ran parallel to the negotiations. As anticipated, it had no effect on them. Sinn Fein refused to attend any of the meetings of the Forum, and the SDLP walked out in July, barely a month after it was established. With nationalists not represented, it turned into a venue for unionist politicians to make statements.

In late May, just after the election, I was contacted by the governments. Would I accept an invitation to serve as chairman of the plenary sessions in the talks? Tony Lake had notified me earlier that the governments were interested in me, so I had had time to think about it and discuss it with Heather. I had just one question:

"How long will it take?"

"We can't say for certain, but our best estimate is no more than six months. You should easily be home by Christmas."

"I'll do it."

Nothing was said about any opposition to me. Wrapped in a cocoon of naiveté, I flew to Northern Ireland expecting an easy, noncontroversial entry into serious negotiations. I could not have been more wrong.

CHAPTER 5

"No. No. No. No."

O N June 6, the governments completed the arrangements for the talks, then scheduled to begin on June 10. These included a series of documents which set forth in considerable detail how the process would begin, how it would move into substantive issues, and the rules by which it would be governed. They had previously published the "Ground Rules for Substantive All-Party Negotiations." They now added "Procedural Guidelines for the Conduct of Substantive All-Party Negotiations," a "Scenario for the Opening Plenary Session," an "Agenda for the Opening Plenary Session," and "Terms of Reference for a Proposed Sub-Committee on Decommissioning."

Included within these arrangements was my appointment as chairman of the plenary sessions of the negotiations. Holkeri and de Chastelain were to serve as well. It was with genuine warmth and enthusiasm that we were reunited. I now became aware that there was some opposition to me, so I decided to publicly say as little as possible. I didn't want to get into a personal dispute with those who opposed me. I issued a brief statement accepting "the invitation of the British and Irish governments. I will meet my responsibilities in a totally fair and impartial manner. It is my hope that this process will lead to lasting peace and reconciliation."

Of the ten political parties eligible to participate in the talks, seven supported me and two were opposed; the Ulster Unionist Party made no commitment. As often happens in politics, the critics, although a minority, got the press attention. Paisley led the opposition. McCartney said that he was not opposed to me personally, just to my being "imposed" by the governments. The Ulster Unionist deputy leader, John Taylor, was negative. He told the press that putting me in charge of the talks "was the equivalent of appointing an American Serb to preside over talks on the future of Croatia. . . . [It] is a non-runner."[1]

More significant to me was Trimble's silence. Paisley and McCartney were the leaders of their parties. They were outspoken in their opposition. Trimble could have made it impossible for me to assume the chair by joining them in outright disapproval. But he didn't. He held his fire. His motive was twofold.

He felt, and said publicly, that if I were denied the chair after I had been invited to serve by the British and Irish governments, and with the full support of seven of the ten eligible political parties, the peace process would collapse and the unionists would be blamed. If the process was to fail, Trimble did not want unionists, and especially his party, to be held responsible.

He also wanted to use the controversy surrounding me to achieve a goal more important to him. All of the unionists were adamantly opposed to the "Ground Rules," "Procedural Guidelines," "Scenario," and other proposals made by the governments for the conduct of the negotiations. The proposals included the granting of substantial discretionary powers to the chairman. Trimble, along with the other unionists, felt these proposals should be scrapped. He wasn't opposed to me; he was opposed to my having the authority the governments proposed to give me. He wanted the parties to begin with "a blank sheet"; they themselves would then decide on the rules, the agenda, and the powers of the chairman. He withheld his support for me until he achieved that objective.

Trimble felt that there was an advantage in having a chairman willing to act independent of the governments, even though serving at their invitation. There was a feeling, widespread among the political parties in Northern Ireland and expressed often to me, that the chairman in the last negotiation, Sir Ninian Stephen, the former governor-general of Australia, had been too close to the British government. The parties had been reassured by the performance of the International Body on Decommissioning. They believed that Holkeri, de Chastelain, and I could be trusted to be independent in fact as well as in name.

On June 10, the prime ministers came to Northern Ireland to open the negotiations. The talks took place in an undistinguished British government office building located in Stormont, a suburb of Belfast. There, in a huge estate atop a hill, sits the magnificent building used by the Parliament of the now-long-defunct government of Northern Ireland. It was regarded by nationalists as a symbol of unionist domination. For that reason, the talks did not take place in the empty Parliament but were held, instead, in an adjacent office building.

The statements by Major and Bruton were positive and well received. However, Major and Bruton then left, and problems immediately surfaced. There were two discordant notes. Although ten political parties were eligible to take part in the negotiations, one—Sinn Fein—was not present. Outside, before a huge throng of reporters and television cameras, Gerry Adams led a group of fifteen Sinn Fein delegates up to the locked gate, where they were denied entry. The legislation enacted by the British Parliament to authorize these negotiations was clear: until there was a renewal of the IRA cease-fire, Sinn Fein could not participate in the talks.

The other problem was the chairmanship. When the meeting began, Patrick Mayhew was presiding. My two colleagues and I were across the hall, in Mayhew's office, listening to the proceedings over a closed broadcasting system. We stayed there for two days, while my role was being discussed—a strange experience. Both governments were painfully embarrassed, having believed that the opposition could easily be overcome. But it was proving to be more difficult and messier than anticipated.

Mayhew and Dick Spring repeatedly apologized to us, saying they would understand if we chose to leave, but that they hoped we would stick it out to the end, although they couldn't be certain of the outcome. No one objected to Holkeri and de Chastelain, but the three of us were inextricably linked. Both of them were understanding and supportive.

I told Mayhew and Spring that the peace process was more important than my feelings, and I assured them I would stay until the chairmanship was resolved, one way or the other. Privately, my two colleagues and I were apprehensive. There seemed to be a reasonable chance that we would have to leave before we got started. The worst part was that we had nothing to do. We had already met with all of the parties. I had told them I would be fair and impartial. The only way I could prove it was to serve. Now it appeared that I might not get that chance. It was humiliating, especially for me, but there was no realistic alternative, so we stayed and listened, joking among ourselves about our plight to keep our spirits up.

I woke up the next morning to a flurry of news reports that I was about to step down. Under the headline "Mitchell's role in doubt after day of protest," the *Irish News* reported that:

> The position of former US senator George Mitchell as peace talks chairman was looking increasingly untenable last night as the leaders of the two main unionist parties criticised "the foisting upon them of an unelected chairman by 'despotic' governments."
>
> And a representative of the third major unionist party predicted that Mr. Mitchell would step down before the talks entered their second day.[2]

Since I had no intention of stepping down, I read the story with some amusement, but also with apprehension. Then, after two days and nights of haggling and hesitation, the governments decided that they had to act. It was clear that the DUP and the UKUP would not agree to my serving as chairman. But as the debate unfolded, it had also become clear that much more than that was involved.

No rules of procedure had yet been adopted. If the governments backed down over this issue, a precedent would be established that would give each party a veto over all aspects of the process. There had been no discussion of voting procedures, let alone a decision. But everyone involved understood what was at stake: if unanimous consent was required—if every party's approval was to be necessary for every decision—then this process could not possibly succeed; indeed, it would never get off the ground.

So shortly after midnight on Tuesday night, Mayhew told us that we were "going in." It sounded uncomfortably as though we were embarking on a military invasion of foreign territory. At 12:32 a.m. on Wednesday morning we entered the meeting room. It was a bizarre scene.

Several tables had been put together in the shape of a square with a hollow center. On the side closest to the door through which we entered were seats reserved for the chairmen and the governments. I noticed that a British official was sitting in my chair. He waited until I was almost on top of him before he got up. He quickly explained to me that he had "protected" my seat from Paisley's and McCartney's people. Evidently, the governments feared that the DUP and UKUP would occupy my seat and refuse to leave, requiring their expulsion by force. That would further delay the proceedings and cause a public furor. So a British official was assigned to my seat until I got there. As I sat down and listened to that story, my unease grew.

On the right side of the table were the unionists. When I entered the room and walked toward my seat my attention was drawn to the DUP section by a noisy commotion. There, Dr. Paisley was standing and saying, in a loud voice, "No. No. No. No." He repeated it over and over again, until I was in my seat. Before I could say or do anything, Paisley launched a blistering attack on the governments for "imposing" me as chairman. He then led his delegates in a walkout. They were immediately followed by McCartney and the UKUP people.

I was extremely uncomfortable. I had a fleeting urge to get up and go home and leave these contentious people to their feud. But that was quickly overtaken by the realization that I and the peace process were being tested. If I ran away now, I would be a quitter; more importantly, this process might collapse, with all of the dread implications that had for the people of Northern Ireland. As I looked around the room and saw the eyes of all of the delegates on me, I realized I was being measured.

Although I had read and heard a lot about Paisley and his tactics, this was my first direct exposure to them, and it was shocking. I was accustomed to rough-and-tumble political debate, but I'd never experienced anything like this. But to the other participants in the talks, it was all familiar.

Ian Paisley had been ordained a minister on August 1, 1946, when he was twenty years old. It is reported that after the ceremony a prominent evangelist said, "I have one prayer for this young man, that God will give him a tongue like an old cow. Young man, go into a butcher's shop and try and run your hand along a cow's tongue; it's as sharp as a file. Please God this man will have a tongue that shall be as sharp as a file in the heart of the enemies of the king."[3] If ever a prayer was answered, it was that one.

At six feet three inches tall, with a huge frame and a deep, booming voice, Paisley is an imposing figure. He was later described by his son as a "firebrand orator," an accurate description. According to Dennis Cooke, a Methodist minister whose book, *Persecuting Zeal*, analyzes Paisley's religious writings and sermons in detail, Paisley's preaching, from his early days on, has been anti-Catholic and sharply critical of those Protestant churches willing to engage in ecumenical dialogue.[4]

Paisley described Pope John Paul II as "anti-Christ, the man of sin in the church."[5] And he said of those Protestant clergymen who he felt had strayed: "apostate ministers are pimpled clergymen, pimpled with questioning, they are broken out in a rash of unbelief, they are covered in boils of scepticism, they are consumed with fevers of ecumenism, they are blackened with the blackness of popery."[6]

Such heated rhetoric attracts attention, and Paisley increasingly got attention as a minister. At the same time he was attracted to and drawn into politics, eventually winning election to the British Parliament in 1970 and to the European Parliament in 1979. As Northern Ireland slid into the violence of the Troubles in the late 1960s and 1970s, Paisley established himself at the intersection of religion and politics. From there he held forth, becoming the dominant figure in unionist politics, although he never served the executive task of governing, preferring to remain on the outside, in opposition.

Paisley's career has been marked by dramatic, headline-grabbing events: demonstrations, counterdemonstrations, rallies, marches, walkouts, picketing, and various other disturbances. He served two brief terms in prison, both of which increased his fame and his support. His political objective is for Northern Ireland to remain within the United Kingdom, and he has repeatedly attacked British prime ministers for what he sees as their sellout of the union. In 1969, when Prime Minister Harold Wilson appointed Shirley Williams as minister of state, Paisley said:

It is quite evident that Mr. Wilson is following closely a policy which he intends will lead to our destruction. Mrs. Shirley Williams is a member of the Roman Catholic lobby at Westminster, and her first loyalty, as a devout Roman Catholic, must be to the Pope and the Roman Catholic Church. As the Pope and the Church are bent on the destruction of Ulster Protestantism, she will no doubt pursue with vigor the official policy of her church.[7]

In 1985, after Prime Minister Margaret Thatcher entered into the Anglo-Irish Agreement, Paisley attacked her in a Sunday sermon at his church: "O God, in wrath take vengeance upon this wicked, treacherous, lying woman."[8] After John Major signed the Downing Street Declaration, Paisley told him, "You have sold Ulster to buy off the fiendish republican scum."[9] More recently, Paisley has consistently accused Major and Tony Blair of being liars. He called Blair "the greatest aider and abetter of the destruction of the Union that Dublin and the IRA have ever had."[10]

Almost all of the major political figures in Ireland—north and south—have been criticized by Paisley, none more harshly than other unionist politicians. He declared that James Molyneaux, the former leader of the Ulster Unionist Party, was a "Judas Iscariot."[11] He was consistent in referring to David Trimble, Molyneaux's successor as leader of the UUP, as "Judas," and then added, for good measure, a "traitor" and a "loathsome reptile."[12]

Such rhetoric has served several purposes for Paisley. It has kept him constantly in the news; media everywhere are attracted to politicians willing to make colorful and controversial statements. It has intimidated his opponents, many of whom appear to believe that they cannot win a name-calling contest with Paisley. It has earned him the intense devotion and loyalty of his supporters. And, over time, the consistency of his rhetoric has brought him a certain tolerance even from those in Northern Ireland who disagree with him; a common reaction to a Paisley outburst is "Well, that's just the way the Doc is." Whether one agrees or disagrees with Paisley's views and tactics, there can be no doubt that his words and actions appeal to and speak for a sizeable part of the unionist community.

President Bill Clinton reaches through a crowd to shake hands with a boy in a Belfast neighborhood, November 30, 1995. Clinton's visit to Northern Ireland marked the first by a sitting U.S. President.   (Reuters/Win McNamee/Archive Photos)

Bill Clinton and John Hume, leader of the mainly Catholic Social Democratic and Labour Party, react to a crowd chanting "We want Bill," outside the Guild Hall in Londonderry, November 30, 1995.

(AP/Wide World Photo)

Clinton meets with Sinn Fein President Gerry Adams during a reception at
Queen's University in Belfast, Northern Ireland, November 30, 1995.

(AP/Wide World Photo)

OPPOSITE: John Major, center, flanked by Northern
Ireland Secretary Patrick Mayhew, left, and Irish
Prime Minister John Bruton, opens the multi-party
talks on the future of Northern Ireland in Belfast, June
10, 1996. (AP/Wide World Photo)

British Prime Minister John Major leaving 10 Downing Street, London, to make a statement to Parliament, February 12, 1996, about the February 9 IRA bombing at London's Docklands business area.
(AP/Wide World Photo)

George Mitchell talks with fellow members of his commission, Canadian General John de Chastelain (left) and former Finnish Prime Minister Harri Holkeri, June 9, 1996, on the eve of the multi-party talks. (Reuters/Martin McCullough/Archive Photos)

The Reverend Ian Paisley, right, walks through the RUC lines on Drumcree Road, Portadown, Northern Ireland, after talking to police chiefs. The RUC prevented the Orange church parade from marching Sunday, July 7, 1996, through the mainly nationalist Catholic area of the Garvaghy Road.

(AP/Wide World Photo)

Protestant marchers near Portadown check out the police presence as they are blocked off for the fourth day by police barbed wire, July 10, 1996.

(AP/Wide World Photo)

Newly appointed Northern Ireland Secretary Marjorie Mowlam arrives in Belfast, May 3, 1997. Following the British Labour Party's election victory, Mowlam was appointed as the top government official in the troubled province. (AP/Wide World Photo)

John Hume, left, Irish Prime Minister Bertie Ahern, center, and Gerry Adams read a statement to the press, July 25, 1997, at the Government Buildings in Dublin after their first joint meeting following the Irish Republican Army cease-fire.   (AP/Wide World Photo)

OPPOSITE: Democratic Unionist Party members Nigel Dodds, left, and Peter Robinson, right, leave the multi-party talks at Stormont Castle over a row for decommissioning terrorist weapons, July 16, 1997.   (AP/Wide World Photo)

Ulster Unionist spokesperson Ken Maginnis re-enters the
Northern Ireland peace talks in Belfast, October 7, 1997.
(AP/Wide World Photo)

Marie Trainor, aunt of Damien Trainor, is visited by David Trimble, left, leader of the Ulster Unionist Party, and Seamus Mallon, right, of the Social and Democratic Labour Party, March 4, 1998, at her home in the village of Poyntzpass, Northern Ireland. Trainor's nephew, a Catholic, and his Protestant friend Philip Allen were shot dead in a bar the previous night.   (AP/Wide World Photo)

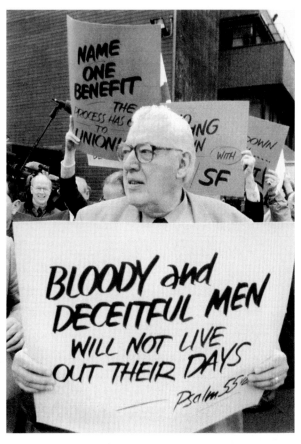

Ian Paisley leads a group of protesters, March 23, 1998, to Stormont Castle after Sinn Fein was allowed to rejoin the peace talks.
(AP/Wide World Photo)

David Trimble talks with reporters, March 30, 1998, as the peace talks enter their final stage with two weeks to go. At right is UUP member John Taylor.

(AP/Wide World Photo)

Gary McMichael, center, leader of the loyalist Ulster Democratic Party, during a pre-talks news conference at Stormont Castle, April 6, 1998.

(AP/Wide World Photo)

David Trimble, right, talks with British Prime Minister Tony Blair at Hillsborough Castle near Belfast, April 7, 1998. Blair flew to Northern Ireland after the major Protestant party rejected a draft peace accord. (AP/Wide World Photo)

Loyalist demonstrators protest outside Hillsborough Castle, April 7, 1998.
(AP/Wide World Photo)

OPPOSITE: David Trimble, bottom, left, crosses the path of Gerry Adams, right, outside a press room at the Stormont Castle, April 8, 1998. Trimble refused to talk directly to Adams since Sinn Fein gained admission to the peace talks in September 1997 following the cease-fire. (AP/Wide World Photo)

Bertie Ahern, right, with Irish Foreign Minister David Andrews, speaks on his return to Northern Ireland after attending his mother's funeral, April 8, 1998.
(AP/Wide World Photo)

George Mitchell formally announces that all parties in the peace talks have approved a historic deal, April 10, 1998. His associate Martha Pope is seated behind him.

(Reuters/RTV/Archive Photos)

David Trimble speaks to reporters at the end of the talks, April 10, 1998. (AP/Wide World Photo)

Martin McGuinness and Gerry Adams comment on the settlement, April 10, 1998.   (AP/Wide World Photo)

Bertie Ahern and Tony Blair shake hands, April 10, 1998.
(AP/Wide World Photo)

Bertie Ahern, George Mitchell, and Tony Blair pose together after signing the peace agreement, April 10, 1998.   (AP/Wide World Photo)

Heather, Andrew, and George Mitchell

Now, after Paisley and McCartney had led their parties out of the talks, the remaining delegates watched to see if I had been intimidated by the demeaning and unruly controversy over the chairmanship. Realizing what was at stake, I tried to remain calm, to avoid betraying the swirling doubts I felt. I slowly made an opening statement. I thanked those present for their support, especially the governments. They had invited me to serve as chairman, and they had stuck with me. I then tried to lift the level of discussion. I reminded the delegates of the huge and important issue which had brought them together: the pursuit of peace and political stability in Northern Ireland. I again pledged to act in a fair and impartial manner and assured them that my only interest was to be helpful to them and to the people of Northern Ireland. I couldn't tell what effect my remarks had on those listening, but they helped me to calm down and gave me a few minutes to establish myself.

I felt that it was important that something be accomplished at this first meeting other than my assuming the chair. The governments had required that any party wanting to participate in the negotiations had to pledge compliance with the Mitchell Principles of democracy and nonviolence. So I announced that I would ask each party, then and there, to make clear its total and absolute commitment to the principles. I made up a procedure on the spot. I read the principles aloud and then called on each government and party to affirm its commitment. The British secretary of state, the Irish foreign minister, and the leader of each of the seven political parties present did so. The process was underway.

It was, to say the least, an unpromising start. I was supposed to preside over negotiations involving two governments and ten political parties, a complicated enough task. But two of the parties were so opposed to my serving as chairman that they had stormed out in protest, while another party was outside trying unsuccessfully to get in. Not for the last time, I wondered how I could ever get them to agree on anything of substance when they couldn't even agree to sit together in the same room.

I was anxious to get the process moving. So, although we had been in session into the early hours of Wednesday morning, I convened a meeting later that same morning. When it began, the two parties that had walked out the previous night, the DUP and the UKUP, were not present. I had talked with Paisley and McCartney earlier in the morning in an effort to persuade them to return. They were agreeable, despite their earlier harsh words.

Just before noon, Paisley came into the room, accompanied by his deputy, Peter Robinson. I welcomed them and told Paisley that I would now ask him, on behalf of his party, to affirm its commitment to the Mitchell Principles, which I then read out. Paisley responded with a speech in which he called the entire process a "complete charade" and criticized the Irish government. He then accepted the principles without reservation. I thanked him and said that I regarded his additional comments as personal remarks which did not affect his party's acceptance of the principles.

That afternoon, McCartney and his deputy leader, Cedric Wilson, joined the meeting and accepted the principles. It was ironic, I thought, that the DUP and the UKUP would accept the Mitchell Principles while opposing Mitchell. But I didn't betray any emotion, and neither did they. The important thing was that they were inside the process. Only Sinn Fein was still out. Hopefully, the IRA would resume its cease-fire and Sinn Fein could come in, which would make it a fully inclusive process. But, at the time, we didn't know if or when that would happen, so we had to proceed.

The chairmanship had been settled, and the Mitchell Principles had been accepted. But some of those who had walked out and returned now vowed they would not call me "Mr. Chairman," thus refusing to acknowledge that I had any authority. So they called me Senator, which didn't seem like much of an insult to me. In any event, what mattered was that they were inside the room. Besides, as I told my colleagues, I had been called a lot worse. So when they called me Senator, I simply smiled and said nothing. Gradually, they came to accept me, and more and more of them started calling me Mr. Chairman. Over time, our relations became cordial, many of them using my first name in private meetings even as they continued their public opposition to me.

The next meeting was scheduled for the following Monday, so I decided to accept an invitation to attend a tennis tournament at the Queens Club in London, hoping to get a break from the tension in Belfast. My host was Frank Lowe, an advertising executive. After a pleasant lunch with him and some of his other guests, I went out to watch the tennis. Just a few minutes after I took my seat, I was approached by Richard Evans. Richard is one of the top tennis writers in the world, and a longtime friend of Heather's. When I saw him walking toward me I thought I'd hear the latest news of the tennis tour. Instead, he greeted me by asking: "Have you heard about the bombing in Manchester?"

The IRA had exploded a large bomb in Manchester. Richard related the brief account he had picked up off the wire service in the press room. As we were talking Lowe came up to say that news of the bombing and of my presence had already circulated at Queens, and several reporters, some with television cameras, had gathered to get an interview. I knew little of what had happened, and I didn't want to grant any interviews until I had gotten a full briefing. Lowe helpfully arranged for a car to take me to my hotel, where I quickly checked out and went to Heathrow Airport for a flight back to Belfast.

When I arrived my staff provided me with all of the available information. A large bomb had devastated the city center in Manchester. The IRA had claimed responsibility. Holkeri, de Chastelain, and I immediately issued a statement: "We strongly and unequivocally condemn today's bombing. This reprehensible act comes at a crucial time, just days after multi-party talks began. We believe that the way to peace is not through violence, but rather through meaningful dialogue." It was the first of many such appeals we were to make over the next two years.

In a society with a long history of politically motivated violence, a negotiating process was always vulnerable to those who opposed it and who sought to destabilize it. I felt it important to establish early and repeat often my conviction that those opposed to the peace process could not disrupt it through the use or threat of violence; to permit that to occur would be to hand over to the men of violence control over the future of Northern Ireland. They had to know—and the people had to know—that there was a democratic alternative available and that it would continue to be available, notwithstanding the efforts of those who chose war over dialogue.

At the Monday meeting, all of the participants strongly condemned the bombing. They didn't know why the IRA had acted when and as it did. But their comments made it clear that if the bomb was intended to help get Sinn Fein into the talks, it had the opposite effect. The attitude of the British government toward Sinn Fein hardened; it would be a long time before they entered the talks.

By general agreement, the first order of business was to adopt rules of procedure; then there had to be agreement on an agenda for the remainder of the opening plenary session of the negotiations. It should have taken a few days. It took seven weeks. There were many disagreements over the rules, but there were two basic conflicts.

The ground rules, and the related documents agreed on by the British and Irish governments, were opposed by the unionists because they felt they were based on earlier agreements by the governments—the Anglo-Irish Agreement of 1985, the Downing Street Declaration of 1993, and the Frameworks Document of 1995. These British-Irish agreements included provisions which the unionists believed threatened the union and could lead to a united Ireland. For precisely those reasons, the Irish government and the nationalists favored their adoption, without change, as the rules of procedure for the negotiations.

The second basic conflict was over my authority as chairman. Since the DUP and the UKUP had failed to prevent me from becoming chairman, they now tried to deprive me of any authority. Except for the UUP, the other participants wanted a chairman with substantial authority. Had the UUP joined the DUP and the UKUP in outright opposition, it's doubtful that I could have been seated as chairman; so the UUP could (and later often did) say that they were instrumental in my being seated. But having me as chairman was one thing; having me as a chairman with broad authority was quite another. So they searched for words and phrases that would limit my authority.

For several weeks the participants debated the rules. In the end, the precise words had little effect on the negotiations. The unionists prevented the ground rules and the related documents from being adopted intact, and they kept out of the rules of procedure what they regarded as the most offensive provisions of the ground rules.

Trimble's tactics had worked. As he explained, "What I did achieve was to open up the procedures and instead of continuing on the agenda designed by the two governments we are now adjourned for a week during which a committee will draw up fresh procedures and re-examine the agenda."[13]

I felt throughout the discussion that ultimately my ability to be effective would depend more upon my gaining the participants' trust and confidence than on the formal description of my authority. I had learned this in the Senate, where the position of majority leader was not created by the Constitution or by law. It started as a practice, then became a custom. Although a modern majority leader has certain defined powers, ultimately his influence is based on his ability to persuade his colleagues. That in turn is based on how much they respect and trust (or fear) him.

The discussions were long, often continuing late into the night. It was a tedious and arcane debate. For example, does the chairman have more or less authority if he makes a decision after "consulting with" the participants, or "having regard" to their views, or "having due regard" to their views? I didn't know the answer before the lengthy discussion, and I didn't know it after.

The tediousness of the talks was relieved somewhat by the fact that Heather joined me in Belfast. We had planned for her to stay there with me for the month of July. But a new crisis developed which interrupted Heather's visit and threatened the talks.

Three thousand parades are held in Northern Ireland each year, most of them by Protestant organizations. The marches have a deep emotional and symbolic significance for many Protestants, who view them as celebrations of their heritage and identity, and as vindicating their right to peaceful assembly. But Catholics believe they have the right to be free from the triumphalism of Protestants marching through Catholic neighborhoods to celebrate the Protestant military victory in 1690 which, in the Catholic view, led to centuries of discrimination and humiliation.

The overwhelming majority of the parades take place peacefully, usually following discussions between representatives of the two communities at the local level. But no such discussion has taken place for the best known and most controversial of all parade locations: Drumcree Church in Portadown. The route takes the marching Protestants down the Garvaghy Road, alongside which live hundreds of Catholic families.

In the last few years, on this one day in early July, at this small

church, along this otherwise ordinary road, there had been erup-
tions on both sides of the pent-up resentments, the smoldering hatreds, the accumulated grievances of centuries past. Emotion had
overwhelmed reason, and what little there was in Northern Ireland
of a willingness to compromise had vanished.

The march was scheduled for Sunday, July 7. But before it began,
Hugh Annesley, the RUC chief constable, announced that the
marchers would not be permitted to take their traditional route
down Garvaghy Road. Fearing widespread public disorder, Annesley insisted that the procession be rerouted.

The unionist reaction was immediate and furious. Trimble accused Annesley of having made a "grossly irresponsible" decision.[14]
The head of a prominent Protestant organization told a huge crowd
assembled at the site that "if we fail in this you can rest assured that
we are finished."[15] Appeals were made to unionists to come to
Drumcree to join "the siege." Thousands responded. Each day the
crowd grew larger. Each night Northern Ireland was torn by violence. Cars, trucks, and buses were burned. Homes were fire-
bombed. Roads were blocked. The society was slipping toward
anarchy.

The press told the story dramatically. Typical was a huge headline
in one Belfast newspaper: "FURY." Under it the story said:

> Ulster shuddered to a standstill last night as a massive explo-
> sion of loyalist protests sealed off towns and blocked major
> roads across the Province. Vehicles were hijacked and burned
> by angry mobs at dozens of flashpoints where police and secu-
> rity forces were overwhelmed by the sheer number of protes-
> tors who took to the streets in the thousands. During serious
> rioting in north Belfast Roman Catholic families were forced
> to flee from their homes and a number of people were injured
> during running battles between rival factions.[16]

The *News Letter* that day reported another ominous development. A thirty-one-year-old Catholic taxi driver, Michael
McGoldrick, had been killed the night before, shot in the back of
the head. Three days earlier, McGoldrick had graduated from
Queen's University with a degree in English and high hopes. He

and his wife had a seven-year-old daughter, and his wife was expecting their second child. His murder sent a shuddering question through Northern Ireland: Was the loyalist cease-fire over? If so, the prospect loomed of a renewal of widespread sectarian war.

Prime Minister Major responded to the escalating crisis by ordering two additional battalions of troops to Northern Ireland. It had become obvious that the rioting and violence was beyond the capacity of the RUC to control.

On Thursday Annesley reversed himself. The RUC, which had been preventing the march from proceeding, now forcibly moved the Catholics out of the way so that a thousand Protestants could parade down Garvaghy Road. The nationalist reaction was predictable. The principal nationalist newspaper, the *Irish News*, summed up their attitude with a large, single-word headline: "BE-TRAYED."[17] As unionist rioters victoriously left the streets, they were replaced by grim and angry nationalist rioters.

It took several days for the fever to burn itself out. Immense damage had been done. Hundreds of homes and vehicles were burned. Thousands of visitors left, and many more who had planned to come cancelled their reservations. More ominously, the harsh rhetoric and the orgy of violence raised anew the question of whether there could ever be any accommodation between two communities so badly riven by fear and hate.

Annesley explained in the *Guardian* that "we had reached the stage this evening and tomorrow when potentially tens of thousands of Orangemen stood to face thousands of policemen and soldiers. The risk to life in those circumstances, accidental or otherwise, was too great to face."[18] The problem, of course, as the same article made clear, was that Annesley was "effectively admitting that loyalist violence . . . had paid off."

Annesley now had the worst of both worlds. He was seen by the unionists as having bad judgment for initially insisting that the parade be rerouted, and by the nationalists as being weak for reversing that decision under the pressure of mob violence. It was unfair to him, since most people believed that the decisions had been made by his superiors. Within months, his term completed, he was gone.

As the riots raged, the peace process hung by a thread. We met on the afternoon of Tuesday, July 9, two days after Annesley's initial decision and two days before his reversal. The mood was tense. I began by suggesting that, in view of the ongoing events, each party should, if it wished, suggest how we could best proceed. When I asked if that was agreed, a DUP delegate said it was not. He harshly criticized the British and Irish governments, blaming them for the crisis, and said that his party was withdrawing from the talks until the Drumcree situation was resolved. A UKUP delegate said much the same thing. Then the delegates from both parties got up and walked out. We had been in talks for less than a month, and these two parties were walking out for the second time.

An intense discussion followed. It was obvious that no progress could be made in the talks in the current circumstances. But all of the remaining parties wanted the process to continue; they feared that if there were a lengthy adjournment the talks might never resume. I decided that the best approach would be to continue the process but to have the meetings in bilateral form, two or three parties meeting together or with the chairman. There would be no large meeting in either a plenary session or in "informal discussions" until I felt it would be productive to have one. In that way, the process could continue. We adjourned that afternoon subject to my recalling them.

Holkeri, de Chastelain, and I then issued a statement in which we said, in part:

> We recognize the extreme difficulties of the talks now underway, especially in the current climate. We have consulted with the participants. There was a clear consensus among them to continue with the talks and to do so with a sense of urgency and increased determination. We will do all we can to further that objective. We remain convinced that the solution to the problems so evident during the past week lies in dialogue and in the resolution of differences around the negotiating table.

We wanted to keep the process alive; but as we left Stormont that day we didn't know when, or if, we would meet again.

When the violence erupted, the security services advised that Heather leave Northern Ireland. We were especially concerned because she was pregnant. So we accepted their advice, and she left immediately. I joined her in London a few days later, and then returned to Belfast to make an assessment. After consulting with Holkeri and de Chastelain, with the political leaders and with government officials, I called a meeting of all of the participants for Monday, July 22. There would by then have been a break of nearly two weeks, and, in my judgment, the situation on the outside had calmed down enough to permit a resumption of the talks.

The meeting was long and very contentious. The DUP and the UKUP returned, along with all of the seven other parties. The delegates hurled insults and invective at each other. I had learned a valuable lesson about the fragility of the process and the sensitivity of the participants to external violence. The memory of this day was with me nearly two years later when, fearful of the effects of a new surge of violence, I decided to propose a final, rigid deadline for the talks.

For now, the process held together. I was able to steer a little of the discussion to the subjects that were supposed to be under consideration: the rules of procedure and the agenda for the remainder of the opening plenary session. But the parties remained divided on several key issues. Near the end of July I became concerned when I learned that the participants expected that the talks would be recessed for the month of August whether or not agreement was reached on the rules. I wanted badly to go home, to spend at least part of August in Maine with Heather, but I was worried that if the talks recessed after two months without being able to reach agreement on the rules of procedure, they might never get off the ground.

I considered threatening to keep the participants in session in August as a way to force a decision. I had used the tactic in the Senate, usually successfully. But when I discussed it with officials of the two governments and with some of the party leaders, they warned me against it. As one of them told me, "It may have worked in the Senate but it won't work here. They'll just laugh at you and leave anyway." I accepted his advice.

In a series of private meetings with key party leaders, Holkeri, de Chastelain, and I encouraged them to work their differences out, and we suggested compromise language. We told them we would be willing to decide, in the way we thought fair and most likely to produce agreement, those issues on which they couldn't agree. We would then prepare, in time for the next meeting on Wednesday, a document we hoped they all could accept. They narrowed the differences to four provisions. Holkeri, de Chastelain, and I decided on those four. We then prepared and circulated to the parties what we hoped would be an acceptable final document.

But before they got to discuss it, someone leaked it to the press—the first of many leaks. I quickly learned that leaks were an integral part of this negotiating process. All of the participants sought to advance their positions inside the negotiations by manipulating the press outside. Whatever the result from the standpoint of the parties, it made the process of negotiation much more difficult. Countless hours were to be consumed by attacks and counterattacks, accusations and recriminations, over what had appeared in the morning newspapers. It didn't just take up a lot of time, it poisoned the atmosphere, creating and exacerbating hostility among the participants.

Despite the leak, Wednesday and Thursday were busy and productive days. We spent a lot of time on the proposed agenda for the remainder of the opening plenary session, and we tried to figure out how to enact the rules if and when agreement on them was reached. The fact that we had spent weeks debating what the rules should be was an explicit acknowledgment that we were operating without rules. The proposed rules contained a complex voting procedure called "sufficient consensus." It required four separate tests for approval of any measure—the support of parties which together represented at once a majority of the overall electorate and a majority from within both the unionist and nationalist communities, based on the results of the May election; it necessitated the support of a majority of the political parties present, with each party getting one vote; and it required the approval of both governments (except for Strand One matters, which were within the exclusive jurisdiction of the British government). It was intended to be, and was in fact, a mechanism which ensured that any agreement reached in the talks would have broad support. It also created four separate vetoes. No proposal could survive a negative vote cast by either government, or by the UUP, as the largest unionist party, or by the SDLP, as the largest nationalist party. I remember thinking to myself: I thought it was tough to pass anything in the Senate. But compared to this process that was easy.

The existence of such a provision in the proposed rules immediately raised an obvious question: Should this voting process be used to approve the rules? I thought the answer should be yes, and so did most of the participants. That raised a further question: Should we vote separately on the rule which included the process, and then on the other provisions, or should we vote on the whole package at once? How these questions were answered would determine whether the proposed rules would be approved.

A year later, in July 1997, when Sinn Fein was about to enter the talks, the DUP and the UKUP walked out for good, vowing to "wreck the process." But in the summer of 1996, they had not yet reached the point where they were overtly trying to wreck the process. They constantly criticized the British and Irish governments. They opposed and challenged me. They made life politically difficult for David Trimble and the UUP. But they participated in the process, and at times they made what I thought were constructive suggestions.

On Wednesday afternoon, the DUP asked to see me. At the meeting Peter Robinson spoke for them. Robinson is a member of Parliament, intelligent and articulate, an effective advocate for his party. Even those who disagree with him respect his ability. He proposed a complex procedure under which the proposed rules would be voted on section by section, beginning with sufficient consensus, and then, in a concluding vote, as an entire package. Under sufficient consensus, even if the DUP and the UKUP voted no, the package would be approved if the Ulster Unionists and the loyalist parties voted yes; combined, they represented a majority of the unionists. The advantage of this proposal, from the DUP's standpoint, was that they could vote for some provisions they favored and then vote against the entire package. The advantage from my standpoint and that of those participants who wanted the process to move forward was that the rules of procedure would be adopted and we could proceed to substantive negotiations. This seemed to me to be a reasonable compromise.

Then Robinson added another condition: that the voting on the rules occur on the following Monday. This created a problem for me. Some of the other parties were expecting immediate action. They wanted to force a vote on the entire package as soon as possible. I knew they would be adamantly opposed to any delay.

We went back into session on Wednesday evening. We were approaching agreement on the rules of procedure and the agenda for the remainder of the opening plenary, when suddenly a new controversy erupted. Did this group have the authority to make any decisions?

After initially constituting itself as a plenary meeting, the participants had decided that the detailed talks would be "informal discussions" among themselves: the same people, the same room, the same subject matter. It was hard to differentiate a formal plenary session from an informal discussion. Nonetheless, the argument raged: some urged that even though they were meeting in informal discussion, they had the authority to make decisions and should do so immediately, that evening; since the plenary consisted of the same people, any decision made tonight would inevitably be ratified at the next plenary session scheduled for the following Monday. Others argued that there was an important legal distinction between a formal plenary and an informal discussion, and that in the latter format there was no authority to make any decision; nothing could happen until Monday. This debate, begun on Wednesday evening, went on through the next day.

All I wanted was to get the rules and agenda adopted. How and when were less significant, so long as they were agreed to before we broke for the August recess. By Thursday evening, after consulting with Holkeri and de Chastelain, I concluded that waiting until Monday, as originally suggested by the DUP, was the method most likely to achieve agreement. So I announced my decision to that effect just before we adjourned at about 8:30 p.m.

I had just gotten back into my office when some members of the SDLP came in. They were upset. They had thought we were going to press ahead and vote this week, tonight if possible. They were concerned that Paisley would use the weekend to rally opposition to the rules and as a result, Trimble would end up voting against them on Monday. How could I fall for such an obvious ploy? I repeated my belief that this way the rules were more likely to be approved;

bulling ahead to vote tonight or tomorrow, without any agreed outcome, left the result in doubt. But by the time the discussion ended, I'd begun to doubt my judgment.

My doubts increased dramatically when, in the privacy of discussion with our staffs, every member of our staffs opposed our decision. They felt that Holkeri, de Chastelain, and I had caved in to those who opposed us and abandoned those who supported us. I had great respect for all of them; their unanimous opposition caused me grave concern. Although it was after midnight when I got back to my hotel room, I was so worried that I couldn't sleep.

I replayed again and again in my mind the meeting with the DUP, the full meeting, the later discussions. Should I have done anything differently? Could I have *said* anything differently? I had sided with those who had walked out over my becoming chairman and who were opposed to the process, and acted against those who had supported me and who wanted this process to succeed. Was that a betrayal? Or was it right to accept the most sensible proposal, whatever its source? But, then again, was it the most sensible proposal?

The telephone rang, interrupting my thoughts.

"Hello."

"George, this is Janet." It was my brother's wife.

"Janet! What's the matter?"

"Robbie's in very bad shape."

My brother Robbie had been diagnosed with bone marrow cancer several years earlier. His spleen had been removed, he received a blood transfusion every two or three weeks, and he regularly underwent uncomfortable and inconvenient treatments. Through it all his spirits had remained high, at least outwardly, and he was able to travel and keep busy. Now Janet was calling to say that he had taken a sudden turn for the worse, and was weak and bedridden.

Our family has always been very close. My brothers, Paul, Johnny, and Robbie, and my sister, Barbara, all had settled in our hometown of Waterville, Maine. I was the only member of our family who had left Waterville, but I returned at every opportunity. We spent long, enjoyable evenings together, playing cards, arguing about politics and sports, kidding each other and laughing. For me it was a form of therapy, a bit of relief from the pressures of the Senate. Robbie and I were close in age, born just twenty months apart, separated by one year in school. We grew up together, he the older brother who was a prominent athlete, who always had money and a girlfriend, I the younger, frail brother who was lousy in sports, hardly ever had a date, and worked for Robbie to earn spending money. In his senior year, Robbie led Waterville High School to the state title in basketball and was chosen the most valuable player in the championship game. In my senior year, I was unable to make the varsity team. That accurately summed up the difference in our status. I looked up to and loved him.

Later in life, after I entered the Senate, I often told the story of how Robbie taught me an important lesson in life. When he was a junior in high school and I was a sophomore, he was already a successful entrepreneur, with a number of small business ventures. Like most of our classmates, every afternoon and evening during the school year we went to the Boys Club to play, mostly basketball. The Boys Club closed at nine o'clock each night. One evening, Robbie approached me with a business proposition. He said he had gotten "the concession" to do the janitorial work at the Boys Club; if I were willing to help he would split the fee with me. I didn't know what it meant to get a concession, but it sounded important, so I quickly accepted his offer. I had worked for Robbie before. It was a good source of spending money.

At nine o'clock he handed me a broom and told me to sweep all of the floors, dust the desks and chairs, empty the wastebaskets, and clean the bathrooms. While I was working he went into the director's office, sat in the director's chair, put his feet up on the desk, and talked on the telephone with Janet, who was then his girlfriend. When I cleaned the director's office I had to be quiet so as not to disturb him. By ten-thirty I went into the director's office to report to him that I had finished. He said good night to Janet, hung up the phone, and we went home.

This went on for a week, at the end of which he paid me $2.50. I thanked him and thought about how lucky I was to have such a smart and generous brother. A few weeks later he told me he had gotten "the concession" to do the janitorial work at a small office building next door to the Boys Club, and he offered me the same deal. I couldn't believe my luck. I already had two other jobs, delivering newspapers in the morning and washing cars at a used-car lot in the afternoon, so with the office building job I would be earning over $10 a week—an incredible amount of money for me at the time.

I had been at it long enough now that I could clean the Boys Club in an hour; the office building took another hour. So Robbie talked to Janet on the phone for two hours every night. I couldn't figure out how they could see each other at school every day and still find something to talk about for two hours each night. But I suppose from Robbie's point of view it beat cleaning the bathrooms.

This arrangement continued for several months. I then learned, by accident, that Robbie was being paid $15 a week for each concession. That meant he was paying me $5 a week while keeping $25. And I was doing all the work. That didn't seem right to me. I screwed up my courage and confronted him. He calmly explained that it took a lot of brains to get a concession; if he hadn't had the brains there would be no jobs for me and I would be out $5 a week. He then used a phrase I'll never forget: "I'm management and you're labor, and management always get paid more." I was still troubled, but I couldn't think of any rejoinder, so I left and continued the arrangement. But I recall thinking, When I grow up I want to be management.

Now, nearly fifty years later, Robbie lay dying at home, and I was in a hotel room in Northern Ireland. Janet put him on the phone, and we spoke briefly. His voice was faint and weak. "George, I love you," he said. "I love you, Robbie," I replied. We said a few more words. I fought back the tears until we hung up. Then I laid down and cried.

I was torn by conflicting demands. I desperately wanted to go home, to see Robbie again before he died. If I leave right now, I thought, I could get to Waterville by Friday evening. But how could I leave now? If the rules aren't approved, would the entire peace process end? Or was I exaggerating the significance of the rules? On the other hand, Robbie is already dying. Even if I see him there's nothing I can do to change that. If I stay perhaps I can help save some other lives? Or is that an even greater exaggeration of my role and of the status of the talks? Was I rationalizing? I didn't know. I couldn't know.

Unable to decide, I picked up the phone and called Robbie's doctor. Richard Stone is a superb physician and human being. At the Dana Farber Cancer Institute in Boston he gave Robbie the best of care, and he gave him more: his friendship. I respected and trusted Dr. Stone. It took a while but I finally reached him in Atlanta and explained the situation. He reassured me. Although there could be no guarantees, people in Robbie's condition usually lingered for four to six weeks, he said. It was unlikely that anything would happen over the weekend. If I could get there by the middle of next week, I should be able to spend a lot of time with him. I thanked Dr. Stone and hung up.

I immediately made up my mind: I would stay until the rules were approved, then I would leave. That way, I could get to Waterville by Tuesday, in plenty of time to see Robbie. *Plenty of time to see him.* I repeated the words to myself several times, trying to convince myself that I was doing the right thing. The doubts lingered. Was Dr. Stone just telling me what he thought I wanted to hear? Or was he sincere but wrong? He was very careful to say, more than once, that there could be no guarantees.

Finally, as dawn broke, I got up to take a shower. I hadn't slept. I had made my decision, but I didn't feel any relief, because I knew that I would never see Robbie alive again. I flew to London and Heather with a very heavy heart.

For the next two days it was hard to focus, hard to do anything but wait with dread for the phone to ring. The call came, finally, on Saturday. He had died that morning.

Heather and I spent the longest and saddest weekend of our life together, in a hotel room in London. There I second-guessed myself and replayed in my mind my life with Robbie. I flew back to Belfast on Sunday evening, once again filled with doubts about being in Northern Ireland. How long will this go on, I wondered? Can there ever be an agreement?

On Monday morning, the participants met. In less than an hour, with brief, unemotional discussion, seventeen votes were held. The rules of procedure were adopted without a hitch. Unfortunately, the parties were unable to agree on an agenda for the remainder of the opening plenary session. But the peace process was still alive.

There were some long-term consequences from this first summer of negotiations, especially from the Drumcree crisis and the fact that the talks survived and even made some progress. The SDLP withdrew from the Forum, never to return. Although some unionists later tried to make the Forum the center of activity and importance, at the expense of the talks at Stormont, they did not succeed. Press coverage of the Forum declined, and public interest in it waned. In the end it had little effect on the process.

I felt a growing acceptance by the participants. We had been together through two difficult months. They had had the chance to see me preside and make decisions. John Taylor had been negative toward me in June. Now, to my surprise, I read: "Talks sources yesterday expressed surprise at the report [that I was threatening to resign] and [UUP Deputy Leader John] Taylor said: 'There hasn't been a whisper about this.' He described Mr. Mitchell as an excellent chairman and added: 'He has shown great ability and tremendous patience and tolerance from the word go.' "[19] I smiled as I thought about my transformation from an American Serb to an excellent chairman, all in less than two months.

I left for the airport immediately after the final vote on the rules to return home to attend Robbie's funeral. Janet had asked me to deliver the eulogy. I had often given such talks, including at my mother's funeral, without ever breaking down. But this time I couldn't finish. I began to falter near the end. I tried to say the words "Good-bye, Robbie," but they wouldn't come. Tears came instead.

The August break was just in time. I had vacationed at Mount Desert Island, on the coast of Maine, each summer for many years. To me, it's the nicest place on earth. The mountains, the forests, and the ocean meet in a setting of spectacular beauty. The August days are warm, the nights cool; the air and water are pure; the scent of the pine forests mingles with the salt smell of the ocean to produce a fragrance that man cannot duplicate.

We spent the month hiking, boating, playing tennis, reading, having long dinners with friends. We had done it all before, but now it somehow seemed better. We knew we had to enjoy this time together, since it was clear that the process in Northern Ireland was going to be much longer and harder than we had thought. But we were also joyous over the fact that Heather was three months pregnant.

Before we were married I wasn't sure about having children. I was sixty-one when Heather and I were married, with a twenty-nine-year-old daughter, Andrea, by my prior marriage. It was one thing to marry a woman twenty-five years younger than me. But to have children? What were my obligations to a child whose father would be in his eighties by the time he or she entered college? And to Heather, who might have to bear the brunt of responsibility for parenting? Her certainty banished my doubts.

So August was a month of restoration, and of reaffirmation of life. My brother had died. I was soon to have a child.

CHAPTER 6

No Progress

I returned to Belfast on September 9, 1996, with high hopes. I was trying not to be naive, but since we had reached agreement on the rules, surely we could now reach agreement on an agenda and get into substantive negotiations.

As soon as I arrived I was contacted by both governments and several of the political parties. They were concerned about continuing press speculation that I was so fed up with all of the bickering that I was about to resign. They asked that I make a public statement restating my intention to remain. I agreed and did so the following day. This was to become a regular practice. On several occasions in the future, as the talks teetered on the brink of failure, speculation would resurface about my imminent departure. Each time I had to go before the press to deny it. Only once did I seriously consider leaving.

When the talks resumed that afternoon, a new obstacle arose. The governments had insisted that every participant in the talks had to pledge to honor the Mitchell Principles. All had done so. But what if a party later violated one or more of the principles, as one was accused of doing now? That was anticipated during the debate on the rules. As a result, one of the rules provided that if an allegation were made of noncompliance with the principles, it would be referred to the governments for decision; London and Dublin were obliged to consider the views of all of the participants.

The rule was silent on the procedure to be followed when a violation was alleged, so I made one up. The allegation was brought by the DUP against the two loyalist parties, the PUP and the UDP.[1]

The participants agreed to my suggestion that after the DUP's written allegation was circulated, the PUP and the UDP would have overnight to prepare a written response. On the following day, after the DUP had a chance to review the response, there would be a full plenary meeting. The DUP would have thirty minutes to make its case; the PUP and UDP would have thirty minutes to respond. There would then be a question-and-answer period during which any party could ask any other party any question. Following that there would be a general discussion. The whole process was not to exceed three hours. Then the matter would go to the governments for decision.

The meeting on Tuesday was long and acrimonious. The DUP and the UKUP argued for the expulsion of the loyalist parties on the ground that the loyalist paramilitary organizations had made public threats of violence. An internal feud had developed among unionist paramilitaries. One of their most prominent figures, Billy Wright, dissented from the CLMC's support for a continued cease-fire. In response, the CLMC had ordered him to leave Northern Ireland or face "summary justice." The DUP and the UKUP stressed that they really didn't want the loyalist parties expelled; they just wanted the death threat against Wright lifted. Most of the other parties favored keeping the loyalist parties in. So did the British and Irish governments. They had been, and still were, trying to make it an inclusive process. The last thing they desired at this stage was to expel participants.

Before the governments had a chance to decide what to do about this matter, a new allegation was made. During the Drumcree crises of July, members of the Alliance Party orally charged several of the unionist parties with violations of the Mitchell Principles; they were alleged to have incited the widespread violence which followed the chief constable's initial decision to prohibit the Protestant parade from going down Garvaghy Road. The Alliance Party now followed up with a written allegation against four of the unionist parties: the DUP, UUP, PUP, and UDP. The initials were still ringing in my ears when I got back to the hotel that night. I had come back the day before and reaffirmed my commitment to the process, hoping to get right into discussions about the agenda. That now seemed a distant dream. I was deeply discouraged.

An insistent ring woke me from a deep sleep. As I reached for the telephone I glanced at the clock. It was just after one o'clock in the morning. Since the hotel operator screened my calls, I knew it would be important. It was Heather.

"Hello."

"I'm sorry to wake you up."

"What's the matter?"

"I feel sick, really sick. I don't know what to do."

My heart sank. It was a call I had hoped never to receive. Heather and I had been elated and then concerned about her pregnancy. Now what we had feared was about to happen.

"Have you called the doctor?"

"I've got an appointment tomorrow afternoon at one o'clock."

I had flown back and forth across the Atlantic so often I knew the schedules by heart.

"I can get to JFK by one. I'll meet you at the doctor's office."

"Are you sure you want to come home? You just got there, and I'm not sure what's wrong."

"I think I should be there."

We talked for a few more minutes, trying to stay calm, trying to sound hopeful. But we both knew that there were painful days ahead.

After we hung up I called a member of my staff. If I caught a 7 a.m. flight from Belfast to London I could connect with a flight that arrived at JFK at 1 p.m.

I had been scheduled to go to London at midmorning for a meeting with Prime Minister Major and other British officials. The meetings would have to be rescheduled. Major would understand.

I tried to go back to sleep but couldn't, so I turned on the light and attempted to read. I couldn't focus on that either, so after a few minutes I got up, got dressed, and went for a walk.

Downtown Belfast was deserted. I followed a familiar route, out past Queen's University. The impression of the city held by most Americans is drawn largely from televised images of burning vehicles and rioting crowds. Those are real events, of course, but they present an incomplete picture of Belfast.

As I looked across the beautifully manicured lawn at the main building at Queens, an imposing structure in the cool wetness of early morning, I thought for a moment that it's too bad Americans can't see this too—it's a more real part of Belfast than the bombs. But mostly, I thought of Heather. I wondered whether I was wrong to be here, walking the streets of Belfast, as she lay sick in New York, alone, going through what must be one of the most difficult nights of her life. Not for the first time, or the last, I asked myself over and over: Should I just leave and not come back? Can I fairly meet all of my obligations when this place is so far from home? What's the right thing to do? The words echoed in my mind. *What's the right thing to do?*

I had plenty of time to shower, dress, and pack before leaving the hotel at 6 a.m. for the trip to the airport. As I boarded the plane to begin the long flight home, I had lots of questions, but no answers.

Heather lost the baby. A few days later she and I walked across the plaza at Lincoln Center. The water from the fountain sparkled in the brilliant sunshine of a warm September day. New York had never seemed brighter, more vibrant, more alive. But we had never felt worse, as we walked, slowly, silently, sadly.

We had talked about it so often that we knew each other's thoughts. Finally, Heather broke the silence.

"You've got to go back."

"Are you sure?"

"Yes, I'm sure. It's the right thing to do. I'll be fine."

How can we *know* what's right? I thought. I don't want to leave her. But I also want to go back. Hopeless as it seems, I believe in what I'm doing. And down deep, I think there's a chance. Through all the killings, all the hatred, all the harsh words; past all the conflicts and obstacles, I believe the people want peace so badly that somehow, some way, they can get there; and I can help.

I feel so grateful to Heather. As she has at every critical moment in our life together, she has understood me and said just the right thing. There was a long pause as I struggled to find the words to say the right thing in return.

"Heather, I promise you, there'll be another chance. We're going to have a baby."

We sat by the fountain. She put her head on my shoulder and cried for a long time.

I returned to Belfast the following week. In my absence the governments had rejected the DUP's allegations against the loyalist parties. Since the Alliance Party's charges against the loyalists were based on the same facts, the governments decided not to take any action on them; they were simply disregarded. Still pending were the Alliance accusations against the DUP and the UUP. So a lengthy debate now occurred on whether or not any other business could be discussed while a decision was pending on a request for expulsion. As a result, no other business was transacted, or even discussed.

A few days later, the governments rejected the Alliance Party's contentions against the DUP and the UUP. But before we could return to the unfinished business of trying to agree on an agenda, a new controversy erupted.

The rules of procedure imposed upon all of the participants a rule of confidentiality. The negotiations were private and were supposed to stay private. The reality was just the opposite. There was usually a large contingent of media just outside the gate, and every day while we were in session many of the participants walked out to the gate to hold press conferences. It quickly became a regular part of the process. In addition, virtually every document prepared during the negotiations was immediately leaked to the media. The only people who observed the rule were the independent chairmen. I believe that was one reason why the three of us gained the respect of the participants.

A lengthy debate took place on the issue of confidentiality. The parties accused each other of violating the rule, and they disagreed on what was covered under it. The result was inconclusive. I closed the debate by suggesting that what was most needed was greater trust among the parties. No one laughed out loud, but as I looked around the room, they were smiling.

CHAPTER 7

An American Interlude

I continued to wonder if these talks would ever actually begin. I had now been there nearly four months, and we still couldn't get agreement on a preliminary agenda. Then I had a reprieve, a welcome break from what looked increasingly like a hopeless effort.

In late July I had received a telephone call from a member of the White House staff. The president and his Republican opponent, Senator Bob Dole, had agreed to two nationally televised debates, to be held in October. The president's staff wanted me to return to the United States for a couple of weeks in early October to help Bill Clinton prepare for the debates. Specifically, they asked that I play the role of Senator Dole in the mock debates that would be the centerpiece of the preparation.

For the six years I had served as majority leader of the Senate, Bob Dole was minority leader. We saw each other many times every working day and became friends. We had many political disagreements, but we never had a personally disagreeable conversation. I like and respect Bob Dole and regard him as a good friend. Our relationship was based on mutual respect and the recognition that, whatever our political differences, we had to work together for the Senate to function.

We had debated each other often, in public and in private. The Clinton team thought that I knew Dole's mind and mannerisms better than anyone else. They also told me that they wanted someone who would not be afraid to say unpleasant things to the president, and they thought I would do that.

It was flattering to be asked, but at the time in the talks we hadn't even approved the rules of procedure, and I didn't think I should leave for the amount of time this would require. It wasn't just the mock debates. There would be travel and a lot of time devoted to preparation. In addition, I had been in Northern Ireland for months and was losing touch with the political situation in the United States. So I declined.

In September I received a telephone call from Erskine Bowles, the president's chief of staff.

"Hi, Erskine. How're you doing?"

"I'm doing just fine, Senator."

"What's up?"

"The president would really like you to help him out, getting ready for the debates with Bob Dole."

I repeated my reasons for declining. He was ready for each of them. The staff had prepared several volumes of background material. They would ship them to me in Northern Ireland. After I read them I could suggest how they could best be condensed. They would reduce to three the number of days that my presence would be required before each debate. And, if I didn't want to attend the actual debates, I didn't have to. They weren't worried about my being out of touch politically. They had plenty of people whose job was to stay in touch.

"Senator, the president and I both think you're the best person to help on this. The debates are going to be critical. We'd like you to do this."

He paused, then concluded: "Senator, the president is sitting here with me. Would you like me to put him on the line?"

"No, Erskine, that won't be necessary. I'll do it."

Well, I thought, at least it will be a short break from having to listen to the same arguments, day after day, in Northern Ireland.

Within a few days I received seven thick, black loose-leaf binders containing everything Dole had said in public in the past two years. It was heavy going, but I read it all. I laughed at my plight. All day long I listened to Northern Irish politicians giving essentially the same speeches over and over again. Then, late into each night, I read the words of an American politician giving essentially the same speeches over and over again. And I wasn't being paid for either. That he was such a good friend made it all the more humorous.

After I had gone through the books I called Steve Ricchetti, the member of the campaign staff who had been given the job of getting me ready to be Bob Dole. I asked him to condense the seven volumes into one, giving the greatest weight to Dole's most recent statements and to those he repeated most often. So the highest priority was given to a statement made the day before by Dole and which he had repeated several times, the lowest priority to a statement made only once or twice, months ago, and not reiterated since.

The system worked well. The one volume I received several days later included almost every word Dole later spoke in the debates; everything he said, Clinton had heard before. It wasn't a particularly difficult or complex system. By the last month of a campaign, the issues and the candidates' views are well known. I assume that Dole was as well prepared, and that he was not surprised by anything Clinton said in the debates.

On Wednesday, October 2, I traveled to Chautauqua, New York, a famous conference center. The inn is old and rustic, oozing charm. The weather was beautiful, a clear and crisp fall day. On Thursday morning I met with Ricchetti and a few other members of the staff who had been assigned to help me. I received several one-page summaries of Dole's positions on key issues that were expected to come up in the debates.

The schedule worked up by the staff called for three full-scale mock debates, one each on Thursday, Friday, and Saturday. Since the actual debate was to take place at nine o'clock on Sunday evening, the mock debates were scheduled each day at that time. During the day, the president and his senior staff discussed the likely questions and proposed answers. Several staff members participated from time to time in these sessions. Among those who were most active were Bowles, who organized and supervised the entire process with his usual efficiency; George Stephanopoulos, Harold Ickes, Mark Penn, and Bob Squier. I was impressed by the skill and foresight with which the process of preparation was organized and implemented. After the first full day I was certain that the president would do well in the debate.

If I had made a judgment based solely on his performance in the first mock debate, I would not have been so confident. On Friday, the president met with reporters and told them that I had beaten him "like a drum" in the first mock debate the previous evening. He laughed when he said it, but he wasn't kidding or exaggerating. He hadn't been fully focused and hadn't had time to get through all of his briefing books. I was fully prepared, having spent most of the previous forty-eight hours getting ready. In addition, I used prepared notes in that first mock debate while the president had none.

I knew from my experience with him that Clinton would improve as he got closer to the real thing. And that's just what happened. If he earned only a 50 percent grade that Thursday night, it jumped to 75 percent by Friday, then to 90 percent by Saturday. By the time he faced Dole and the television camera on Sunday evening, he was as close to 100 percent as a human being can get. That's because he possesses the skills needed for a great debater. He is extremely intelligent. He knows the issues better than any public official I have ever dealt with, and far better than any other president I have met. He has an uncommon ability to describe complex issues in clear, understandable language. And he has a near-perfect sense of timing: if a sixty-second answer is required, he gives a concise, organized answer within that time. I know he has been criticized on occasion for his long, rambling answers at press conferences and in other situations. It's true; he has given those kinds of answers. But in those situations he wasn't time limited. In the debate he was. That restriction served him well. Forced to focus, to be concise, he was at his best in Hartford.

I've known Bob Dole since I entered the Senate in 1980. He is intelligent and courageous, with vast experience in government. Had he been elected, Dole would have been a good president. But he doesn't possess Clinton's debating skills. I had a long-standing business commitment that required me to be elsewhere on Monday morning, so I didn't attend the debate. Just before the president left for Hartford, to give him a boost I told him: "Bob Dole cannot beat you in this debate. You can blow it if you don't stay calm and steady and stick with your game plan. But if you do, it'll be a decisive victory."

I watched the debate on television in a hotel room. Just before it began Heather called me, so we were on the phone when they started speaking on the stage in Hartford. As each question was asked I tried to predict what Dole would say. I was as amazed as Heather was when, on several questions, his answers were virtually word for word what I had just said. In preparation for this debate I attempted to get across Dole's ideas, proposals, and responses in a general way. I wasn't consciously trying to get the precise words. As I watched the first debate unfold, I began thinking about the second debate. This time I would consciously try to anticipate and use the exact words that Dole would use.

The president's keen personal interest in Northern Ireland was again made clear to me in the course of the debate preparation. When I first saw him on Thursday he asked about Northern Ireland. Here he was, three days away from what was arguably one of the most politically significant days of his life, and before we even mentioned the debate we spent half an hour reviewing the status of the peace talks. I was one of several people who had dinner with Clinton in the large dining room at the inn on Friday evening. Once again he turned the conversation to Northern Ireland. He repeated to me, and to the others present, his determination to do all he could to bring the conflict there to an end.

On the day after the debate, after completing my business commitment, I flew to Pittsburgh to attend a trade and investment conference on Northern Ireland organized by the Commerce Department. I was scheduled to speak at a luncheon held at a downtown hotel. As the car pulled up to the curb in front of the hotel, I saw a crowd of reporters waiting for me. I knew in an instant that something was wrong. Before I could get out of the car, a Commerce Department aide got in: I should know before I faced the cameras that a huge bomb had just gone off in Northern Ireland. The first reports were sketchy, but apparently there were some deaths.

The IRA had smuggled two cars, each packed with a bomb estimated to be over 500 pounds, into a British military base in Lisburn. It was widely interpreted as an attempt to provoke retaliation by the loyalist paramilitaries. The next day's headlines in the *Belfast Telegraph* told the story: "Lisburn Bomb: Peace Process Shattered—

Hardliners push loyalist trust to breaking point."[1] But the cease-fire held, thanks in large part to the leadership of David Ervine and Gary McMichael, the leaders of the loyalist parties, who persuasively urged restraint. The talks went on.

Bill Clinton's success in the first debate and other campaign developments placed great pressure on Dole in the second debate. His criticism of the president was becoming increasingly direct as he responded to Republican critics who charged that he had let Clinton off too easy in the first debate. Albuquerque, New Mexico, had been chosen as the site for preparation for the second debate. Just prior to my going to Chautauqua, I had received a telephone call from the president's campaign chairman, Peter Knight. He began by telling me that he had just had a conversation with Hillary Clinton and that he was speaking for her as well as for himself. They were concerned that Dole would be tough on the president in the debate, and worried that Clinton would be unprepared for it because no one would confront him adequately. He said that they had strongly supported the decision to ask me to become involved, reiterating that I would be willing to say to the president the tough things he needed to hear. I assured Peter I would do so. And I did.

Now, as I reviewed the most recent briefing papers on the flight to Albuquerque, I concluded that since Dole was toughening his rhetoric, I would have to do the same, especially since there was increasing speculation in the press that the second debate was Dole's "last chance" to close the gap. I felt I had had just the right tone in preparing for the first debate. But what was right then wouldn't be right ten days later.

We followed the same schedule. Since the encounter was to take place at six o'clock on a Wednesday evening in San Diego, there were three mock debates at six o'clock in the evening on Sunday, Monday, and Tuesday. I hit the president hard in all three. Whitewater, the handling of FBI files, military service, marijuana use, tax increases—I covered them all, and more. I was reasonably certain that Dole would not be as insistently negative and on the attack as I was. But whatever he did eventually say I wanted Clinton to have first heard from me; I wanted him to have thought about it and to have considered carefully how to respond.

There was no beating him like a drum in Albuquerque, as there had been at Chautauqua. The president was calm and reflective, absorbing all the criticism and responding in a way that was truly presidential. Once again, he improved each day. As we left for San Diego, I had no doubt about the outcome of the debate.

Clinton asked me to join him on Air Force One for the trip to San Diego. During the flight Hillary asked if I would sit with her on the stage. Each candidate had two seats reserved for his family. Dole's wife and daughter used his. But since the Clintons' daughter, Chelsea, was at school, one of the seats available to them was vacant. Hillary and I spoke infrequently during the debate, since we were so intent on what the candidates were saying. I thought that both candidates were better than they had been in Hartford. But the result was the same.

Later, when I heard what had happened in the large room behind the stage where the staff was watching the debate on television, I regretted not having been there. Moments after the debate ended, as the candidates talked on the stage with the milling crowd, in a hallway off-stage crowded with staff and security, George Stephanopoulos said to me: "I wish you'd been there with us. Every time Dole gave an answer that was word for word what you'd said, the staff let out a huge roar. It got louder each time. You'd have loved it."

As Clinton made his way off the stage and down the jammed hallway, he grabbed me by the arm and steered me into a nearby men's room. He said, "I want to talk to you." I knew what was coming. Whether a city councilman or president of the United States, public officials need reassurance. In much less important circumstances I'd asked the same question myself, so often that I mentally recited it before he asked it.

"How'd I do?"

"You did very well."

"Really? You think it went all right?"

"Better than all right. I told Mrs. Clinton that you'd just been re-elected."

"Dole was OK tonight."

"Better than the first time. But you were better too."

"You really think it's over?"

"Unless you do something really stupid, which I know you won't, it's over. It's really over."

It wasn't just the campaign that was over. So was my political interlude. A few days later I boarded a plane for yet another trip across the Atlantic, back to a debate that was longer and tougher than the ones I'd just witnessed. And I wasn't at all certain how this one was going to end.

CHAPTER 8

Beyond Reason

O N October 15, the participants had agreed on an agenda for the remainder of the opening plenary session. When I got back to Belfast, I jokingly told Holkeri that I ought to leave more often so that progress could be made. We laughed, both of us knowing how very difficult it was to make any progress.

The agreed-to agenda was a good example. It was less than a page long and general in its wording. In its entirety, it read:

AGENDA FOR REMAINDER OF THE OPENING PLENARY

1. Circulation and Introduction of Proposals regarding the Comprehensive Agenda.
2. Consideration of the International Body's proposal on decommissioning:
   a) discussion of proposals;
   b) participants' commitment to work constructively to implement agreements on decommissioning;
   c) consideration of, and agreement on, mechanisms necessary to enable further progress to be made on decommissioning alongside negotiations in three strands.
3. Discussion and Adoption of Comprehensive Agenda.
4. Launch of three-stranded negotiations and establishment of agreed mechanisms on decommissioning.
5. Concluding remarks by Independent Chairman.

15 October 1996

In most negotiations, it could have been agreed to quickly. Here it had taken four months. But it was progress, of a sort.

The participants were debating the second item on the agenda: decommissioning. In a sense, we were back where we had been before the talks began. A year earlier, the unionists had wanted paramilitary arms to be given up before negotiations could start. Talks had commenced, but there had as yet been no substantive negotiation. The governments had planned on those talks taking place on three principal subjects, or strands, once the opening plenary session was concluded.

Strand One was to deal with Northern Ireland: What institution(s) should be created and policies adopted to provide fair and nondiscriminatory self-governance for the people of Northern Ireland? Strand Two was to take care of north-south institutions: What institution(s) should be created and policies adopted to encourage cooperative action for the mutual benefit of these societies? Strand Three concerned so-called east-west issues: What institution(s) should be created and policies adopted to further British-Irish cooperation?

The unionists now demanded that decommissioning take place before the substantive negotiations in the three strands began. It was the same issue, but further into the process than it had been the year before.

For several weeks the participants struggled over the issue. There were detailed position papers, long oral presentations, tough questioning, barbed debate. Over and over, the question was analyzed and dissected. The discussion was sharp and acrimonious. Harsh and insulting words were spoken. By the end of November, it was clear that there was no consensus.

Then Bob McCartney, leading an effort by the UKUP and the DUP, presented a motion on decommissioning and demanded a vote on it. The other parties objected. They viewed McCartney's motion as a part of the internal struggle within unionism. Throughout the negotiations, McCartney and Paisley made clear their political differences with Trimble; much of what was said at the talks revolved around this intra-unionist conflict. It was the principal subplot to the negotiations, a continuing and increasingly bitter contest for the leadership of the unionist community. Paisley and McCartney were opposed to the very process in which they were participating; they repeatedly called it a farce and a sham. Trimble, on the other hand, plainly wanted to keep it going.

Now Trimble saw McCartney's motion as another effort to end the talks and to inflict political damage on Trimble's party in the process. He and other delegates made those points repeatedly in the debate.

The other parties didn't want the process to break down over this issue. Elusive as it was, they wanted to continue the search for consensus. Most of them had grown impatient with McCartney. In the meetings, several of them tried to get me to cut him off. In private, they gently criticized me for letting him talk so often and so long; they particularly resented it when he strayed off the subject. I rejected their complaints. I believe in letting people have their say. It was important, I told them, not to cut anyone off at this stage. When the right time comes, I said, I'll bring this to a conclusion. But no progress was being made anyway, so what was to be gained by cutting him or anyone else off?

Much later, several newspaper articles, in praising my patience, said that I had once permitted McCartney to speak for seven hours. Those articles were incorrect. Although he talked a lot, in my presence McCartney never spoke for more than two hours at a time, and he did that only rarely.

In response to the other parties, McCartney, aided by the DUP, argued that the fair and democratic way to proceed was to vote on his motion. He believed that there was no consensus on the issue, and that none was possible; a vote on his motion would make that clear and bring the talks to an end.

I was aware of the seriousness of the issue of decommissioning, and I recognized the importance of dealing with McCartney's motion in a fair and responsible way. So I carefully solicited the view of each participant, orally and in writing, before making a decision. I then spent an entire weekend reviewing those presentations, searching for any relevant precedents, and carefully weighing the arguments. On Monday, December 2, I made my decision and put it in writing. I delivered it at the plenary meeting on the next day.

The question I am called upon to decide is whether, in these talks, each participant's right to raise an issue and to insist upon

and obtain a vote on that issue is a right so fundamental, or in-
alienable, that it must be vindicated without regard to the
views of other participants, or to any other consideration.

I reviewed the positions of each of the parties, noting especially
that several had emphasized that we were involved in a political negotiation, not a legislative process. I further noted that even in legislative bodies like the British Parliament and the U.S. Congress
there is no absolute right by a member to get a vote. I concluded
that:

1. Each participant to these talks has the right to raise any
significant and relevant issue of concern to them and to receive
a fair and reasonable hearing on these issues.
2. Such right does not include the absolute right to have a
vote on each issue. That is a matter for the participants as a
whole to decide.

Understandably, the DUP and UKUP were upset, the other parties
relieved. The process would not break down. The search for consensus would continue.

We had hoped to reach an accord on decommissioning by Christmas. After two more weeks of long and unproductive meetings, it
was obvious that no agreement was then possible. On December 18,
when we adjourned, the negotiations were six months old, and very
little had been accomplished. The participants were downcast, the
public was disillusioned, and I was discouraged. Nonetheless, Holkeri, de Chastelain, and I released an upbeat statement and held a
year-end press conference. I tried, as best I could, to sound hopeful.

John Major came to Northern Ireland that day, a traditional pre-
Christmas visit. It was a fortuitous coincidence, since his comments
dominated the news. He was positive about the process and firm in
demanding that the IRA declare a cease-fire. That evening I was one
of several people invited to have dinner with the prime minister. I
sat next to him, and we had a long talk about the status of the negotiations. To me privately, and then in comments to the entire group,
he expressed impatience with the slow pace of the talks. He knew all
of the participants, and he was well informed on the subject. He also

had a tiny majority in the Parliament. At any time the Ulster Unionists could, if they chose to join with the opposition, bring his government down. So his room to maneuver was extremely limited. But within those constraints he was determined to move the process forward. The next day I spent the entire time on the flight home thinking about ways to break the impasse.

We didn't reconvene until January 27. In the meantime, I was again made aware of the often brutal nature of politics in Northern Ireland.

At 8:15 on the evening of December 20, two men, carrying guns and wearing wigs to conceal their identities, entered the Royal Belfast Hospital for Sick Children. They headed toward the intensive care unit, where six-year-old Andrew Dodds, suffering from spina bifida and hydrocephalus, struggled for life. Their target was Andrew's father, Nigel, general secretary of the DUP, who, with his wife, was at Andrew's bedside. The gunmen were spotted by three policemen assigned to guard Dodds. A gunfight ensued in the corridor outside the intensive care room. One officer was injured. A stray bullet reportedly passed through the incubator of one of the children in intensive care. Dodds and his family were unhurt. The gunmen escaped.

How could anyone try to kill a man in the intensive care unit of a children's hospital, thereby risking the lives of sick and helpless children? I wondered if the length and bitterness of this conflict had destroyed the very humanity of people. I was relieved that Nigel and his family were all right. I telephoned him, and we had a good talk. He belongs to a party that strongly opposed me, but this was beyond politics, beyond reason, beyond humanity.

Two years later, just after Christmas 1998, Andrew Dodds died while sleeping. I again telephoned Nigel. We talked about our sons: my Andrew, just a year old; his Andrew, now tragically gone after nearly nine courageous years of life. It was a sad end to the year.

CHAPTER 9

Smear Tactics

THE talks were constantly threatened by violence; that was no surprise, given the history of Northern Ireland. But it was a surprise when the talks were threatened by sex.

In early November, the negotiations were making no progress; as often happened, the discussion had wandered off on a tangent. Some of the unionists criticized the British government for its efforts to get Sinn Fein into the talks. There had been published reports that some British officials had talked with Gerry Adams. Suddenly, one of the UKUP delegates asked me to confirm that neither I nor my colleagues nor our staff were involved in negotiations with anyone outside of the talks; I was specifically asked whether I or any member of my staff had any contact with Sinn Fein.

I looked at Holkeri and de Chastelain. They shook their heads no. I then turned to our staff, in their customary seats right behind us. They all said no. So I responded to the question by saying that neither I, nor my colleagues, nor any of our staff had had talks with anyone outside of the negotiations, directly or indirectly.

Since the IRA had broken its cease-fire in February, London had cut off direct talks with Sinn Fein. They asked us to follow the same policy, and we had complied. Now, nine months later, the British were obviously trying to obtain an IRA cease-fire and get Sinn Fein into the talks. Prime Minister Major held meetings with John Hume, who was in turn meeting with Gerry Adams. As a result, Major was heavily criticized by both sides. Adams accused him of

"PR tactics" and not offering anything new, while Paisley slammed him for "surrendering to the IRA."[1]

The question from the UKUP surprised me. I had worked hard to be fair and impartial. As I've said, I felt it was important to earn the trust and confidence of the participants. When the crunch came I intended to be active in the search for an agreement; I would need their trust then. Did anyone really believe that I would jeopardize all that by conducting secret negotiations, at this early and uncertain stage? Over the next few days, other matters arose and I forgot about it.

Then, on November 27, the issue was revived in an unusual exchange. The minutes of the earlier meeting had been circulated and were in the process of being approved, a routine matter. A UKUP delegate referred to the earlier exchange and said his party wanted it to be made clear that their question about contacts with Sinn Fein was retrospective, as well as relating to the future. My antennae went up. It felt and sounded as though some kind of trap was being set for me. I said that I accepted the comment, but wanted the record to reflect that the question related only to these negotiations; earlier in the year, during the work of the International Body on Decommissioning, we had met with Sinn Fein on several occasions. The UKUP said they accepted my statement. That evening, I thought long and hard about the exchange. Something was happening, but try as I might, I couldn't figure out what it was.

On Friday, the puzzle deepened. In a debate in the Forum, Paisley said, "I want to go further and put on record in this House that I believe that certain people in Mr. Mitchell's office are talking with the IRA."[2] When I heard about that, I again called my staff and asked them if they had had any contact with anyone from the IRA or from Sinn Fein. They all said no.

The following day, at the DUP party conference, Paisley went further: "People who work in Senator Mitchell's office are not to be trusted, for they're friends of leading members of the IRA."[3] Late that night I received a telephone call from Martha Pope. She had just learned that on the next day, Sunday, newspapers in London and Dublin were going to carry front-page stories alleging that she had been having an affair with Gerry Kelly, a prominent member of Sinn Fein. I asked her directly: "Are the allegations true?" "No," she said, "they're not." She told me that she had never met Kelly. She said that if the accusations hurt me or the talks she would leave if I wanted her to; she didn't want to embarrass me or set back the peace process. I told her not to worry and not even to think about leaving. I had complete faith and trust in her integrity and truthfulness. There was not the slightest doubt in my mind. If she said the allegations were false, they were false.

Even though I was expecting the stories, I was shocked when I saw them. Splashed across the front page of the *Mail on Sunday* in London and the *Sunday World* in Dublin was the same story, replete with separate photographs of Martha and Kelly. It says a great deal about the nature of Northern Ireland politics and about the press in the United Kingdom and Ireland.

The newspapers reported that the security services had provided detailed accounts of weekend meetings between Kelly and Martha during which he allegedly wrote romantic poetry for her. They were allegedly monitored while meeting in Northern Ireland and a British intelligence agency was said to be aware of similar meetings in the Republic of Ireland. The articles reported that Kelly had been imprisoned with a life sentence for participating in IRA bombings in London in 1973. He had since been released and now wished to politicize his role.[4]

I and all of the members of my staff had been in the United States for the Thanksgiving holiday. We flew back to Belfast on Sunday. Immediately upon arrival Martha issued a strongly worded denial to the press. I added that the report was "scurrilous," and said, "The allegations are absolutely and totally false. They are a complete fabrication."

Unfortunately, on Monday the Belfast papers repeated and updated the story. The huge headline dominated the front page of the *Belfast Telegraph*: "Mitchell Rejects 'Liaison.' "[5] Equally dominant was the headline in the *News Letter*: "SF Man Denies US Aide Affair."[6] The *Irish News* downplayed the story, although it appeared on the front page.[7]

For Martha, it was impossible not to be concerned. Her name and face were splashed over the front pages of newspapers in the United Kingdom and Ireland in the most lurid way. In the U.S., the *New York Post* leaped in with a banner headline: "Sex scandal perils IRA truce."[8] Through twenty years of serious, thoughtful work, she had established an excellent reputation; now it, and her career, hung in the balance. We met on Monday to consider what to do. She was indignant, angry that something so totally false could be spread so quickly and so widely. She had made up her mind to obtain counsel and to immediately institute legal action against the *Mail on Sunday* and the *Sunday World*.

We were both puzzled by the response of the British government. Instead of directly denying the allegations, they simply referred to my denial. The Northern Ireland Office (NIO) issued a statement:

> We have had an assurance from Senator Mitchell that neither he, his colleagues or his staff have been in contact with Sinn Fein or the IRA. We accept that.
>
> Asked about the MI5 inquiry claims, [the NIO officer] added: "We do not discuss matters of intelligence."

I knew nothing about the matter except for what I had read in the newspapers and what Martha had told me. A British government agency and report were involved, yet they were quoting me in their statement? I spoke to Mayhew. He told me that they (the British government) didn't think there was anything to it, and that they didn't comment on matters of intelligence. He couldn't even confirm the existence of a report, let alone let me see it. It was a very unsatisfying situation. More disturbing was Martha's report that she had been told that several of the journalists who regularly covered the talks had interpreted the NIO statement as encouragement to keep digging on the story; they regarded the statement as classic government doublespeak, an affirmation in the guise of a denial.

There was another disturbing statement by Paisley. On Monday he was interviewed by a reporter, who then wrote: "It was put [by the reporter] to Mr. Paisley that the allegations against Ms. Pope were scurrilous and false, according to Senator Mitchell. 'He had better be careful when the MI5 paper appears. I am suggesting that papers have a habit of turning up.' "[9] His statement suggested that he had seen an MI5 document. Yet neither Martha, whose life was in the process of being devastated by it, nor I could see it; we couldn't even be told if such a document existed. There was only one way to handle this, and Martha chose it: Go to court, where testimony can be compelled under oath.

That same day, under the headline "Mitchell aide may sue over affair claim," the *Irish News* reported that:

> US newspapers were yesterday reporting that Martha Pope, at the centre of allegations concerning a tryst with top Sinn Fein official Gerry Kelly, might sue the *Mail on Sunday*.
>
> The [*Boston Globe*] said some Washington officials were taking the view that the story had been "concocted" by the *Mail*. "Others, however, were worried that rogue elements within the British government had planted it," the *Globe* report stated.
>
> The Boston paper's story also carried the reaction of un-named Irish diplomats including one who was quoted as saying: "this is not about Martha Pope, this is about a smear campaign against George Mitchell."[10]

Martha obtained qualified counsel, and letters went out to the *Mail on Sunday* and the *Sunday World*. They were now on notice: Martha had categorically denied the allegation and was taking the issue to court.

Within days, the *Mail on Sunday* and the *Sunday World* agreed to pay Martha a substantial sum in damages and to print a retraction. On the following Sunday, one week after the initial stories appeared, they each published a retraction.

The *Sunday World*, under the headline "Apology Martha Pope," stated that it had published an article on December 1 that had linked Martha Pope and Gerard Kelly in a romantic liaison as a result of which, it said, Martha's impartiality in the peace negotiations was jeopardized. Now, in its December 8 retraction, the *Sunday World* declared that there was no truth to the story and that it was competely disavowing the accusation. The paper agreed that the alleged lovers had never even met each other. And it revealed that it would pay Martha damages and legal costs as compensation, and it expressed its deep regret to her for the distress caused by the original article.[11]

Of course, the original allegation had been carried on the front page, with headlines. The retraction was in small print, buried on an inside page.

At midweek, John Steele, the director of policing and security in the Northern Ireland Office, while traveling in the U.S., called the allegation "a spurious non-story. I read all the intelligence in Northern Ireland. I never saw anything hinting at anything like that. I never saw anything to support even an allegation."[12] I knew and respected Steele, and appreciated his statement. It raised interesting questions: Why had not some British official made a statement like that on Sunday, when the story broke, or even on Monday? Instead the NIO had issued a statement relying on what I'd said and then refusing to comment on "matters of intelligence." But Steele was the NIO's director of policing and security, and a few days later he had commented directly on the matter. Was this just an uncoordinated coincidence? Did Steele inadvertently (or intentionally) violate NIO policy when he made his comment? These questions in turn raised others: Was this entire incident a British "dirty trick," as some alleged? But what conceivable purpose could they now have to disrupt the process? They were architects of the negotiations and were working hard to keep them going. This theory didn't make sense to me.

Another widely discussed conjecture held that there were those within the British security service who were opposed to the entire peace process and especially to American involvement; in effect they refused to accept their own government's policy and were working to sabotage it. When the prime minister rejected their assessment that Martha was involved, they leaked the documents. I had no way of assessing this theory. I don't know whether any document existed, or whether Paisley had any role in this matter.

Only those directly involved know what happened, and they're not talking. But I do know this: In all of my years in politics, I have never been involved in anything so despicable. A woman who devoted her life to public service had her career threatened by a totally false report that was given worldwide coverage. Only her courage and determination—and the truth—had saved her.

CHAPTER 10

No Turning Back

W E resumed in January 1997. The Christmas break did nothing for the process. From mid-January to early March, in bilateral meetings and plenary sessions, decommissioning was discussed from every conceivable point of view. There seemed to be no way to reconcile the conflicting positions of the participants. The debates had become repetitious, the parties dispirited. To add to the difficulties, the IRA struck again. On February 12, Stephen Restorick, a twenty-three-year-old British soldier, was manning a checkpoint in a rural area of Northern Ireland. A car being driven by a Catholic woman, Lorraine McElroy, stopped; with her was her young son. Restorick leaned in to speak to her. Suddenly, a single shot rang out and Restorick slumped down, dead, shot in the back. Mrs. McElroy, who was injured in the attack, expressed anger at the risk to her son and sorrow for the dead soldier: "I watched that young man dying last night. It was the saddest thing I've ever seen. It was just so awful." Restorick's mother, Rita, although devastated by the loss of her son, said: "I don't want this to be the thing that starts off the Troubles again."[1] She then became a tireless campaigner for peace, appearing on television and radio, making personal appearances to urge restraint. The incident showed again the worst and best of Northern Ireland: a cowardly killer who would shoot someone in the back and risk the life of an innocent baby, and two women, brought together by tragedy, who responded with compassion and eloquence.

There were no differences on Northern Ireland between the British government and the opposition Labour Party. But there were many differences on other issues. John Major had to call an election in 1997, and he chose May 1 as the date. His prospects were not good. Through death, resignation, and the subsequent loss of by-elections his majority in Parliament had all but vanished. His party was badly divided on the issue of Europe. A strong euro-skeptic faction within his Conservative Party wanted a clear rejection by the government of the proposed European currency, while the most prominent member of Major's cabinet, Chancellor of the Exchequer Kenneth Clarke, favored Britain's joining in. Major tried, without success, to keep his party together.

There were differences on Europe within the Labour Party as well, but they were not as pronounced, and having been out of power for sixteen years, Labour was hungrier and more disciplined. So while the Conservatives slugged out their disagreements on television and in the newspapers, the Labour candidates talked about the issues on which they were united.

By early March, it seemed evident that no progress in our negotiations would be possible for a time. Many of the participants were members of Parliament who would have to campaign for their seats. On May 21, just three weeks after the parliamentary election, local elections in Northern Ireland were scheduled. Many delegates would also be candidates in those elections. So on March 5, we adjourned the talks until June. It was a sad and apprehensive leave-taking.

Once again, my two colleagues and I were called upon to combat the negative interpretation that would result from another adjournment—this one for three months—without any progress having been made. We issued a statement describing as positive the agreements on rules of procedure in July and on the preliminary agenda in October. We acknowledged the continuing deadlock over decommissioning, but said:

> We look forward to resuming the negotiations in June with renewed vigor and commitment, and to working with the participants in completing the address to the International Body's proposals on decommissioning. This would enable the negotiations to move to consideration of substantive political issues concerning a new beginning for relationships within Northern

Ireland, within the island of Ireland, and between the two governments.

We had settled into a grim routine. What little progress was made came very slowly. Then, at each break, when there inevitably would be assessments by the press, we were called on to give a positive "spin." It was necessary, but it made me uncomfortable. When I returned to the U.S., for the first time I discussed with someone other than Heather the possibility of my leaving the talks.

It had been a very difficult year. In June there had been the highly publicized and embarrassing controversy over my becoming chairman. In July my brother had died. In September my wife had lost a baby. Nine months had passed since the negotiations had begun, and almost no progress had been made. There appeared to be no prospect of breaking the impasse that had tied things up since October. Even if somehow it could be broken, what conceivable basis could there be to hope for an agreement on substantive issues, given the long and difficult time spent on procedural matters? The longer the process went on, the harder it was to be optimistic.

I had said over and over, in private and in public, that I would stay as long as there was any chance of success, but if I concluded that the situation was hopeless, I would leave. I now had to ask myself that difficult question: Was it hopeless? Had I been deluding myself, over these many months, when I thought that progress was possible?

On the flight home, I worked on a speech I had agreed to give the following week at a dinner in Washington sponsored by the American-Ireland Fund. I would, of course, say some positive things. But I also got across my belief that both sides were contributing to the stalemate, and that both would have to change if there was to be any hope of progress.

The next day I returned to New York to be with Heather. There, a new and compelling factor entered my thinking: Heather was pregnant again. Because of the experience of the previous year, we were both tense and tentative, obviously hoping for the best but fearing the worst. Was it fair to her if I went back to Northern Ireland in early June, when she would be four months pregnant, precisely the time of loss in her previous pregnancy?

Sandy Berger had replaced Tony Lake as the president's national security adviser. I had known Sandy for years; he's smart and able, a good and trusted friend. I told him of my doubts, that I was thinking of leaving. He urged me to stay, at least until August. If I left now, he said, there was a real danger that the entire process could collapse and the war would resume. We discussed it several times, without reaching a conclusion. I also talked about it with my staff, and many times with Heather. I was badly torn, unable to decide what to do. So I did nothing. I'll wait, I thought, and see how Heather is feeling in a couple of months. As to the election, it was becoming increasingly clear that Tony Blair and his Labour Party were going to win; he had organized, and was conducting, a brilliant campaign.

But what really mattered were the people of Northern Ireland. The brutal murders of Michael McGoldrick and Stephen Restorick; the attempt on Nigel Dodd's life; the bombings and the beatings; the savagery of sectarian strife and the hatred and fear it spawned; no one should have to live like that. I was in a position to help. I didn't seek or expect it, but it was a reality. How could I turn away from it now? I had been taught that each human being has an obligation to help those in need; I had preached the same thing to young Americans countless times. Did I really believe what I said? And if I did leave, and the war resumed, how could I reconcile myself to the deaths that would result, deaths that might have been prevented if I had stuck with it? Finally, and most powerfully, what would I tell the child Heather was now carrying when, by God's grace, he or she was old enough to understand, and inevitably asked me about Northern Ireland?

Heather was as torn as I was. She badly wanted me home, but she understood the imperatives that were pulling me away. As always, she was helpful and supportive. Gradually, as spring came and went, our discussions shifted subtly; we talked less about my leaving and more about how to manage my going back in June; we could review the situation in August, when the talks would be in recess and we would be in Maine. That would be the right time and place for this kind of discussion.

During this break I received daily telephone briefings and periodic written reports from my staff. The news was not good. On

March 27 they reported, "The bombs placed on a main north-south rail line in England at Wilmslow, Cheshire, on March 26 presumably mark a return to violence on the British mainland by the IRA and therefore have further dimmed prospects for a pre-election IRA cease-fire."

On April 15:

The steady drumbeat of disturbing incidents continues. The disturbances over the weekend in north Belfast are only the latest in a disheartening series of events. The craven shooting (in the back) of an RUC reserve officer (a 46-year-old mother of three) in Derry/Londonderry pricked the latest speculative bubble about a pre-election IRA cease-fire. The loyalist cease-fire appears to be badly frayed as distinctions between "measured response" (the defused loyalist bomb outside Sinn Fein's New Lodge headquarters) and tit-for-tat seem to fade. Loyalist spokesmen are increasingly circumspect in their projections for the loyalist cease-fire.

On and on the reports went, an unremitting procession of bad news. When I flew back to London on June 1, I wasn't optimistic. But, I thought, there's a new British government, and it just might be able to break the deadlock in Northern Ireland.

CHAPTER II

"The settlement train is leaving."

LABOUR had won in a landslide, as the voters rejected the feuding Conservatives. When the new Parliament convened, Tony Blair had a huge majority and a degree of freedom in Northern Ireland that Major never enjoyed. Promptly displaying the energy and skill that would mark his government, Blair visited Belfast on May 16. It was his first trip outside of London since becoming prime minister, an important gesture that was not lost on the people of Northern Ireland. There, in a balanced and well-crafted speech, he reached out to both unionists and nationalists.

To the unionists he offered the assurance they so much needed: "Unionists have nothing to fear from a new Labour Government. We offer reassurance and new hope that a settlement satisfactory to all can be reached. Northern Ireland is safe in the hands of this Government."[1]

At the same time, he presented Sinn Fein with the opportunity to meet with British ministers, to make clear his desire to bring them into what he hoped would be inclusive negotiations. There would have to be an IRA cease-fire; and, to blunt unionist criticism of his overture to Sinn Fein, if no cease-fire resulted, the talks would proceed without it. In a phrase that was to be repeated often in the coming year, he said to Sinn Fein: "The settlement train is leaving. I want you on that train. But it is leaving anyway and I will not allow it to wait for you. You cannot hold the process to ransom any longer. So, end the violence now."[2]

Blair's speech was well received. Each side saw something in it for them, and Blair's popularity rose in Northern Ireland. It had been impossible to gauge in the general election, since none of the three major British political parties—Labour, Conservative, and Liberal Democrat—organizes successfully in Northern Ireland. The politics of the six counties is so tightly focused on the conflict there, and the society is so sharply divided, that the political parties largely represent one community.[3]

Blair took another important step: he named Marjorie Mowlam as his secretary of state for Northern Ireland. "Mo," as she is universally known, is a skillful, experienced politician, having served for several years as a member of Parliament. But she has a decidedly nonpolitical approach—she is blunt and outspoken, and she swears a lot. She is also intelligent, decisive, daring, and unpretentious. The combination is irresistible. The people love her, though many politicians in Northern Ireland do not.

I found her a pleasure to work with. She made an early, strong impact on the process and proved to be invaluable to its eventual success. She was ably assisted by the new minister, Paul Murphy. A Welsh member of Parliament (of Irish heritage), he was resilient and pragmatic. An affable bachelor with an easygoing manner, he came to be well liked by both unionists and nationalists.

Mo traveled to Northern Ireland as soon as she was named secretary of state and literally dived into the problem, wading into crowds with joy and energy. They knew who she was, as a result of an extraordinary incident during the campaign. Some newspapers had published unflattering photographs of her, with critical comments about her appearance. When it was revealed that she had had a brain tumor, for which she was receiving treatments that caused her face to swell and her hair to fall out, public sympathy swung sharply in her favor. During the campaign, she had been known and liked. Now she became well known and loved throughout the United Kingdom. At times during meetings she would take off her wig and drop it on the table—one of the many ways she had of breaking the tension.

Major, Mayhew, and Ancram had done well in getting and keeping the process going in difficult circumstances. They deserve great credit for their efforts. Now a Labour government brought new people and new energy to the task of completing what the Conservatives had started.

Among the steps taken by Blair to invigorate the process was the setting of a deadline. Actually, all he did was call attention to an existing deadline and pledge to enforce it. The legislation which established the legal basis for the talks provided for the election of delegates to a Forum; from that group each party would select a smaller number to serve as delegates to the negotiations. The legislation specified that the Forum would remain in existence until no later than May 1998. Although the legislation did not specifically provide a date for the conclusion of the talks, since the Forum and the negotiations were inextricably related, Blair correctly concluded that the negotiations would end by May 1998 as well.

This had been one of Sinn Fein's key demands. Blair's decision was widely interpreted as a gesture to its people, an effort to get them into the process, to make the talks truly inclusive. But it was also very important to me. Shortly after the election I received a telephone call from a British official who told me that Blair was anxious for me to stay on as chairman. Knowing there was going to be a deadline was of crucial significance in my decision to remain.

There was another significant result from the election. David Trimble and the UUP did well. They received a third of the total vote and increased their number of seats in the Parliament from nine to ten. Trimble had taken two risks—backing me for chairman and agreeing to a preliminary agenda. For both he had been flayed by Paisley and McCartney. But his actions appeared not to have hurt him or his party politically. Perhaps now he would be prepared to take even bigger risks.

Labour had been out of power for sixteen years, so its leaders hadn't been ground down by the complexity and difficulty of Northern Ireland. They swept into office brimming with energy and determination. But it didn't take long for Mo, Murphy, and their aides to find out what they were up against. The government may have been new, but the problem was not. The talks resumed in June as they had ended in March: stuck on decommissioning. The IRA had not declared a cease-fire, so Sinn Fein was still outside trying to get

in. The DUP and the UKUP were in, but the intensity of their opposition to the talks grew; McCartney called the process a "macabre
joke" and, with Paisley, watched with growing concern as Blair's
government talked to Sinn Fein. They had walked out before and
returned—a year earlier Paisley had said of me, "If he's in I'm out."
I had been in for a year and he was still there. But this time I had no
doubt that he meant it: if Sinn Fein came in, the DUP and the
UKUP would walk out for good. The crucial question was: What
would Trimble and the UUP do? If they joined the DUP and the
UKUP in a walkout, the talks would surely end; they were based on
the premise that there had to be an accommodation between unionists and nationalists, and if the largest unionist party wasn't in the
talks, there could be no credible accommodation.

Through June and into July two separate discussions took place.
The British government, with the encouragement of the Irish government, met with Sinn Fein to encourage an IRA cease-fire and the
entry of Sinn Fein into the talks. Meantime, the negotiations continued, with the unionists expressing their growing anger at the
British–Sinn Fein discussions. The governments had to take into
consideration that if they succeeded in bringing Sinn Fein in, Trimble would be in an extremely difficult political position.

By early July London and Dublin were ready to act. In consultation with them Holkeri, de Chastelain, and I offered a proposal
which sought to satisfy the conflicting desires of the participants.
We called for the governments to set up an Independent International Commission on Decommissioning; it would be ready to act
by the time substantive negotiations began (hopefully!) in September. There would also be a Liaison Subcommittee on Decommissioning within the talks, so the participants could be directly
involved in this aspect of the discussions. These provisions were intended to appeal to the unionists, who wanted action on decommissioning.

The proposal called for substantive negotiations in the three
strands to begin in early September. Sinn Fein would be included,
provided there was a prompt declaration of a cease-fire by the IRA.
These provisions were intended to appeal to the nationalists, essentially giving them what they had long wanted: inclusive negotiations
by a date certain.

Predictably, the proposal met with criticism from the unionists. They repeated their demand that the meetings with Sinn Fein be terminated. Every aspect of the proposal was carefully and critically dissected. The governments listened, negotiated, responded. The proposal underwent change after change; the only certainty was the objective.

The marching season came and went with less violence and disruption than in the previous year. Mo didn't repeat the mistake of the year before. She made a decision and stuck with it: Protestants in limited numbers could march down Garvaghy Road. The RUC forcibly moved Catholic demonstrators out of the way. There was anger among the nationalists; some called for Mo's resignation. But she rode it out, and the storm was soon over. Meanwhile, in the Republic of Ireland, big changes had taken place.

The peace process had begun when the Taoiseach was Albert Reynolds, the leader of Fianna Fail, which was then in coalition with the Irish Labour Party. A dispute on a matter unrelated to Northern Ireland led Labour to switch to a coalition with Fine Gael, and as a result the leader of that party, John Bruton, took the position of Taoiseach; Dick Spring, the leader of Labour, became the deputy prime minister and foreign minister. All three men were deeply committed to moving the peace process forward. From the beginning Spring had been the senior Irish government representative at the talks. He proved himself to be an effective advocate and a skillful negotiator. He was assisted by Nora Owen, the minister of justice, and Hugh Coveney, a minister of state in the Department of Finance. The senior Irish civil servant at the talks was Sean O'Huiginn, who is now the Irish ambassador to the United States. He had devoted most of his adult life to the effort to establish peace in Northern Ireland and as a result he knew the issues and the personalities very well. He made an invaluable contribution to the negotiations.

Hoping to benefit from a strong economy, Bruton called an election in June. Although the talks at Stormont had earlier adjourned for three months to accommodate the British election, the Irish officials had been insistent that there be no interruption in the talks on account of their own election. It was another example of the importance the country's parties attached to peace in Northern Ireland.

But the strategy backfired. A coalition of Fianna Fail and the Progressive Democratic Party (PDP) prevailed, and the Fianna Fail leader, Bertie Ahern, became Taoiseach. His first foreign minister, Ray Burke, left office after a short while and was replaced by David Andrews, a veteran Fianna Fail member of the Irish Parliament. He headed the Irish talks team in the final months, assisted by Minister of State Liz O'Donnell, a PDP member of Parliament. When O'Huiginn left the talks for Washington, he swapped jobs with Dermot Gallagher, who, along with Andrews and O'Donnell, did an outstanding job. Gallagher developed a good personal and working relationship with several unionist delegates; these relationships would prove to be helpful in the difficult last few weeks of negotiations. The Irish team also benefitted from the participation of Martin Manseragh and David Donoghue. Manseragh is a long-time Fianna Fail foreign policy advisor, close to and knowledgeable about the republican movement. He provided Ahern with valuable advice and insight. Donoghue was the Irish head of the Joint British-Irish Secretariat in Northern Ireland. He knew the people and the politics there well, and he put that knowledge to good use in the negotiations.

Blair and Ahern now had the opportunity to enter the history books as the men who brought peace to Northern Ireland. In both cases, they owed that opportunity to their predecessors, who had begun the peace process and kept it going. Blair and Ahern quickly developed a warm personal relationship and an ease and candor in working together that would prove to be essential to the agreement reached on Good Friday.

CHAPTER 12

Sinn Fein Comes In

O N July 20 the IRA announced a cease-fire. This put David
Trimble in a difficult position, since Sinn Fein would now be
eligible to enter the talks. The DUP and the UKUP had made it
clear that they would permanently leave the negotiations if Sinn
Fein came in, and some members of Trimble's party took the same
position. In a long headline, the *Independent* described Trimble's
dilemma: "Will he stick his neck out for peace? David Trimble has
made some radical moves in his checkered career in loyalist politics.
But now the leader of the Ulster Unionists faces his most critical
decision."[1]

Not only the unionists were divided, as the *Times* of London
reported:

> A leading Sinn Fein official said yesterday that his party would
> accept an interim peace accord that fell well short of the united
> Ireland for which the IRA has fought for the past quarter
> century.
>
> The statement by Mitchell McLaughlin, Sinn Fein's chair-
> man, seemed certain to fuel the significant opposition to the
> renewed IRA cease-fire among rank-and-file republicans, and
> could encourage defections to breakaway groups that have not
> set aside their arms.
>
> The Irish Republican Socialist Party, the political wing of
> the Irish National Liberation Army (INLA), issued a state-
> ment mocking the cease-fire. It asked: "Has the past 27 years
> of struggle against repression, imprisonment and death all

been aimed at securing seats for nationalists at a revamped Stormont and the copper fastening of partition?"

It called the peace process a "thinly-veiled attempt at pacifying nationalist demands while neutralising republican resistance to the British occupation of Ireland," and claimed that view was shared by "a vast majority of grassroots republican supporters and activists."[2]

Trimble and Paisley went to London on successive days to meet with Prime Minister Blair. Paisley urged Blair to scrap the talks and insisted he would leave for good if Sinn Fein were let in. Trimble, by contrast, said, "We are not in the mode of walking out."[3] Of course, for Trimble, walking out at this point was an undesirable option; it would confirm that Paisley and McCartney had been right all along and would render meaningless (or worse, naive) his earlier efforts to keep the process alive. But he couldn't just agree to talks with Sinn Fein. So he negotiated with the governments to make their proposal less offensive to unionists, and he bought time by announcing that the UUP would use the rest of the summer to consult with party members and the public. For the time being, that got him out of the vise many felt the IRA had put him in.

In the negotiations, the debate resumed with increased intensity. The issues were the same as they had been for months: Should Sinn Fein be admitted without a prior handover of arms by the IRA? When could substantive negotiations begin? The three constitutional parties representing the unionist community (the UUP, DUP, and UKUP) insisted on prior decommissioning. The two loyalist parties (the PUP and the UDP), although also representing the unionist community, maintained their opposition to the prior handover of arms because of their affiliation with the loyalist paramilitary organizations. Although the IRA and the loyalist paramilitaries had fought on opposite sides throughout the Troubles, they were united in their opposition to prior decommissioning.

The other parties favored decommissioning but did not want its absence to cause the negotiations to end. They hoped to continue the search for some way to accommodate the UUP, thereby enabling the substantive negotiations to begin on schedule. They knew it would be impossible to satisfy the DUP and the UKUP. The position of those two parties was clear: If Sinn Fein came in, they would leave.

The issue reached a crisis point in a long plenary session on July 22. London and Dublin offered a plan to deal with decommissioning and to permit substantive negotiations in the three strands to begin in September. There was heated discussion. The unionists harshly criticized the governments, bitterly accusing the British of making unprincipled concessions to terrorism. The DUP and the UKUP also attacked the UUP for what they saw as a forthcoming "sell-out of the Union" by Trimble. The other parties accused the DUP and the UKUP of intransigence and of trying to wreck the peace process. The governments vigorously defended their efforts, asserting that they were trying to keep the process going and get substantive negotiations underway in September. Dozens of amendments were offered, and a total of thirty-seven proposals were voted on. In the end, all were rejected; nothing was approved. In the final vote on their proposal, the two governments were joined in support by four parties: Alliance, Labour, the Women's Coalition, and the SDLP. The UUP, DUP, and UKUP voted against; the two loyalist parties abstained. So not one of the five parties representing the unionist community had voted for the governments' proposal.

The rejection should have caused a round of handwringing and general discouragement. But it did not, in large part because of a sense of relief that the process was still alive. The DUP and the UKUP walked out, never to return. But while the UUP had voted no, Trimble said he wouldn't walk out, creating the hope that somehow this obstacle could be overcome. There was, on balance, reason for hope.

The major paramilitary organizations on both sides still were holding their fire. The governments had announced their determination to get to substantive negotiations in the three strands in early September. If Sinn Fein came in and the UUP stayed, the process would reach a new stage of inclusiveness (even without the DUP and the UKUP); the UUP was, after all, the largest unionist party and, together with the two loyalist parties, could be expected to represent effectively the interests of the unionist community.

The headline of an *Irish Times* editorial captured the prevailing view, "A Setback Not A Disaster."[4]

Merely continuing the talks had become an important objective. There was a broad consensus that if they ended without an agreement there would be an immediate resumption of sectarian violence, possibly on a scale more deadly than ever before; the loyalist parties repeatedly made this point with emphasis. Given their relationship with paramilitary organizations, and their importance in maintaining the loyalist cease-fire, their words were taken seriously. So, in effect, the participants in the negotiations believed that they had to keep talking.

On July 28 the talks adjourned until early September. During that six-week period, Mo Mowlam would monitor the IRA cease-fire. If it proved durable, Sinn Fein would be admitted to the talks in September. As I spent August in Maine with my family, the question of what Trimble and the UUP would do was never far from my mind.

The decision by Paisley and McCartney to quit the talks was predictable. It was so much a part of their rhetoric, so deeply ingrained in their political convictions, that there could be no doubt about their intention. Yet, if their objective was, as they repeatedly insisted, to end this process, then their walkout was a fateful error. Reaching agreement without their presence was extremely difficult; it would have been impossible with them in the room. From June 1996, when the talks began, until July 1997, when they left for good, Paisley, McCartney, and their colleagues made life miserable for Trimble and the UUP. Both Paisley and McCartney are skillful debaters (as is Peter Robinson). They spoke often and at length in the negotiations, and, over time, they became more aggressive and outspoken in their criticism. They regularly offered amendments which put the UUP on the spot politically. The long and acrimonious debate over decommissioning kept boiling over into criticism of Trimble and the UUP. No one can ever know for certain what might have been, but I believe that had Paisley and McCartney stayed and fought from within, there would have been no agreement. Their absence freed the UUP from daily attacks at the negotiating table, and gave the party room to negotiate that it might not otherwise have had. To their credit, when the time came, the Ulster Unionists rose to the occasion.

When the talks resumed on September 9, the UUP and the loyalist parties were not in the room. Since the DUP and the UKUP had left for good in July, that meant there were no unionist parties present. Sinn Fein was in, but the talks could hardly be described as inclusive. The London-Dublin policy had been to get an IRA cease-fire and permit Sinn Fein's entry while holding the loyalist cease-fire and keeping the unionist parties in the talks. So the governments and the independent chairmen were now working hard to coax the unionists back in. The UUP and the loyalist parties were trying to figure out how to do that without provoking a politically unacceptable backlash in the unionist community. It was a difficult and delicate task.

The first order of business on September 9 was to obtain Sinn Fein's commitment to the Mitchell Principles. That took place without incident. I then welcomed Sinn Fein into the talks and told them that I looked forward to their active participation in the negotiations.

It had been a long journey for Gerry Adams. Born in 1948 into a large family of active republicans, Adams was raised in the Catholic west side of Belfast. His father, also Gerry, was jailed for five years as a result of his political activities, after which he had difficulty finding a steady job. At the age of seventeen Adams left school to go to work as a bartender to help support his family. He was inevitably drawn into republican politics, his interest sparked by a widely publicized event in West Belfast. The local Sinn Fein office one day ignored the law prohibiting the public display of the Irish flag in Northern Ireland. After considerable debate and publicity, the RUC took it down. The next day it went up again; the RUC lowered it again. Demonstrations and riots followed; fifty civilians and twenty-one policemen were hospitalized. "The impact of these events on me," Adams later wrote, "was to encourage me to become politically curious."[5] Since then his life has been one of political activity.

As violence flared across Northern Ireland in the wake of the civil rights actions of the late 1960s and early 1970s, the Belfast government initiated a policy of internment, under which persons suspected of terrorist activities could be arrested and held without charge or trial. (After that government was dissolved, the British continued the practice.) Adams, by then a prominent local leader, was interned in March 1972. He was released a few months later to take part, with other republican leaders, in secret talks in England with the secretary of state for Northern Ireland, William Whitelaw. But the parlays went nowhere and a brief cease-fire collapsed with a renewal of sectarian violence. In July 1973 Adams was again interned and this time he was held for four years. As has happened so often in so many societies, his imprisonment deepened his commitment to the cause for which he was incarcerated. Released in 1977, he was arrested in 1978 and charged with being a member of the IRA. After seven months of confinement the charges were dismissed.

He then began the long, slow process of transforming Sinn Fein from a political pariah to a mainstream party. To that end he applied his considerable talents: political skill, eloquence in the spoken and written word, and above all else a relentless determination in the pursuit of his objectives. Wounded once in an assassination attempt, he has lived much of his adult life on the run. Yet he has survived, even flourished, in the face of setbacks that would have defeated most men. Unionists deeply mistrust him, labelling him a terrorist and a principal author of the violence of the past quarter century; as Adams is quick to reply, no such charge has ever been proven. There can be no doubt that he is a charismatic leader of a substantial segment of the nationalist community.

In 1978 Adams became a vice president of Sinn Fein and the next year John Hume was chosen the leader of the SDLP. The two men had never met but their lives were on courses that would inevitably intersect, with profound consequences for nationalism in Northern Ireland. In 1983 Adams was elected president of Sinn Fein, a position he has held since. In 1993, following several years of dialogue between Adams and Hume and their parties, an initiative by the two leaders emerged. They set as their goal the creation of a peace process which would involve all parties. They called for a move away from conflict and toward reconciliation, and they accepted that national self-detemination was a matter for the Irish people through agreement. Adams was now poised to make the leap from a local political leader to a world figure. Bill Clinton made it possible.

A transforming step in Adams's journey was the decision by Clinton to grant him a visa in 1994 to enter the United States. That validated Adams and gave him access to the world stage. It led, in turn, to the IRA cease-fire of August 1994. Adams was the recognized leader of the republican movement. He had met with Hume, with the prime minister of the Republic of Ireland, and with officials of the British government. His application for a visa to enter the United States presented Clinton with a difficult decision. The Irish government, U.S. Ambassador to the Republic of Ireland Jean Kennedy-Smith, and many Irish-Americans urged the president to approve the application. They argued that it would enhance Adams's stature, enable him to persuade the IRA to declare a cease-fire, and permit Sinn Fein to enter into inclusive political negotiations. I was one of several senators who signed a letter to Clinton endorsing that view. But the British government, the U.S. State Department, the U.S. ambassador to the United Kingdom and some members of Congress argued vigorously against the visa. They believed that granting Adams a visa would be to reward terrorism. But Clinton approved the visa and, as subsequent events demonstrated, he was right. Adams's trip to the United States was followed by the IRA cease-fire, which paved the way to inclusive negotiations.

It took three long and turbulent years for Adams to get to the negotiating table. But finally, there he was, sitting with the British and Irish governments and many of the political leaders of Northern Ireland. Eventually he had a huge impact on the outcome. But, for unionists, the question remained: Was Adams sincere about committing to exclusively democratic and peaceful methods of political debate, or was this just another tactic in the long-term republican strategy of the armalite and the ballot box? Although many unionists disagree, I believe he is sincerely trying hard, in difficult and dangerous circumstances, to bring his supporters into the grand tent of democracy.

London and Dublin had, on August 26, signed an agreement for the establishment of an Independent International Commission on Decommissioning. This was part of the governments' scheme which had been rejected in July. Although the unionists had voted against the proposal, they strongly supported this provision. So the governments, in a continuing effort to accommodate the unionists, had agreed to form the commission.

The governments' original plan, in June 1996, had been for de Chastelain to chair Strand Two of the negotiations and for me to chair the decommissioning commission. Early in 1997 de Chastelain suggested to me that we swap those assignments; he thought that the decommissioning process best suited his military background while the political nature of the Strand Two talks was more appropriate for my background. Besides, it was likely that decommissioning would extend beyond the time when agreement was reached, if that ever occurred; he was prepared to stay indefinitely, and he knew that I was not. I told him it was all right with me, if the governments and the parties approved. He spoke with them all, and they agreed. It proved to be a beneficial change, because the UUP liked him. Their security spokesman, Ken Maginnis, had a lot to say on the subject of decommissioning, and he had an especially high regard for de Chastelain. When the governments announced the membership of the commission, the unionists were pleased.[6]

The talks were alive, Sinn Fein was in, and there was a widespread expectation that the UUP and the loyalists would soon return. The prospects for the future were better than they had been since the talks began. But in Northern Ireland there always seemed to be setbacks after gains, and that proved true once again.

Sinn Fein publishes a newspaper, *An Phoblacht* (Republican News). In its September 11 edition, just two days after the talks resumed, there was an interview with an IRA spokesperson, which the paper described in these words: "In the first interview since the IRA cessation of 20 July, a spokesperson for the IRA leadership gives an assessment of the political climate in advance of all-party talks." In the interview there was included this exchange:

AN PHOBLACHT: Sinn Fein has affirmed the Mitchell Principles. Do you have a view on that and what of your own view on the Mitchell Principles themselves?
IRA: Sinn Fein is a political party with a very substantial mandate. What they do is a matter for them. But I think all republicans should understand and support them as they do what they believe is right and necessary to bring about a lasting

peace. Sinn Fein's stated commitment is to secure a peace settlement which both removes the causes of conflict and takes all
the guns, British, republican, unionist, nationalist and loyalist,
out of Irish politics. The Sinn Fein position actually goes beyond the Mitchell Principles. Their affirmation of the principles is therefore quite compatible with their position. As to the
IRA's attitude to the Mitchell Principles per se, well, the IRA
would have problems with sections of the Mitchell Principles.
But then the IRA is not a participant in these talks.

The interview caused an immediate uproar. As I have said, outside
Sinn Fein and the IRA themselves, very few people in the United
Kingdom or in the Republic of Ireland accept their claim that they
are separate. The governments say they have overwhelming evidence to the contrary, and the public simply accepts their close relationship as fact and shrugs off their denials.

Tony Blair and Bertie Ahern reacted strongly to the IRA statement on the Mitchell Principles. Ahern called it "a matter of major
concern. I expect the Mitchell Principles to be honored by the entire Republican Movement."[7] Blair said that no one should be naive
about the IRA and Sinn Fein, since the two organizations were inextricably linked. If the Mitchell Principles were violated by any return to violence by the IRA there should be no doubt that Sinn Fein
would not be able to stay in the negotiations.

The IRA statement created two new complications in the talks.
The first was accurately captured by the *Irish News*, in an article
on September 11 headlined "Unionists react with fury to IRA
strategy."

Ulster Unionists may delay entry into next week's all-party
talks after the IRA yesterday distanced itself from Sinn Fein's
acceptance of the Mitchell principles. The UUP's executive
meets tomorrow to make a final decision on attending the negotiations which begin on Monday. However it is understood
the party will postpone its attendance until Sinn Fein's position
is clarified.

A furious Ulster Unionist leader David Trimble yesterday
described republican leaders as "scoundrels."[8]

Another problem greeted me when I arrived at Stormont the next morning, in the form of a letter from Ian Paisley, demanding, on behalf of the DUP, that Sinn Fein be expelled from the talks. So when the talks resumed on September 15, instead of the long-awaited substantive negotiations, there was instead a discussion on whether the DUP had legal standing to bring such a charge. It had left the talks in July. The rules did not contemplate such a situation. On the substance of the allegation, the other parties present challenged Sinn Fein on the IRA statement. Adams repeated his denial: Sinn Fein spoke for Sinn Fein, not the IRA. Sinn Fein had committed to the Mitchell Principles, and it intended to honor that commitment.

The debate was long and confusing and, in the end, inconclusive. But a serious enough question had arisen that I felt compelled to make a statement. Just before adjourning I told the participants that Holkeri, de Chastelain, and I took the principles of democracy and nonviolence seriously and as essential to the success of this process. They represented not just the views of three of us who had devised them and written them down; but, more importantly, they symbolized the aspiration for peace, political stability, and reconciliation of the overwhelming majority of the people of Northern Ireland. If those principles failed, so would the talks. I told the participants that they knew better than I how historic our opportunity was. They could not let the talks fail. And if they were to have any chance to succeed, the principles of democracy and nonviolence had to be honored.

The governments had devised another motion in an effort to finally break the logjam and begin substantive negotiations in the three strands, and they were working hard to get it approved. The principal elements of the motion were: the establishment of the independent commission to verify decommissioning; the creation of the subcommittee of the plenary to deal exclusively with decommissioning; the completion and approval of a final agenda for the negotiations; the beginning of a series of meetings by a business committee to establish a time schedule and procedures to be used in the three strands; and the actual launch of negotiations in the three strands.

We had hoped to accomplish this by September 15. But once again, we couldn't get it done on schedule. There were too many issues still in dispute, especially decommissioning. The Ulster Unionists wanted to see arms handed over, or at least a specific timetable when they would be handed over. The governments could do no more than reaffirm their commitment to decommissioning and set up the mechanisms to achieve it. Would that be enough for the UUP? They had Paisley and McCartney on the outside, daily accusing them of selling out the union. Then again, they had the public (at least through opinion polls) urging them to stay in the talks.

We worked all Tuesday morning to satisfy the concerns of the UUP over decommissioning. Good progress was being made. The governments prepared to brief the other parties during the day, and there were strong indications that the UUP and the loyalists would come in that day. But just before noon a bomb destroyed the center of the town of Markethill. When I heard the news my heart sank and I thought, Oh God, this is so difficult! Every time we're on the verge of progress, a bomb goes off or someone is shot. Will we ever be able to work it out?

The bomb made headline news across the United Kingdom and Ireland. The *Guardian* on September 17 was representative:

> The all-party peace talks on Northern Ireland's future were thrown into disarray yesterday after a bomb ripped through a Protestant village minutes before the Ulster Unionists were preparing finally to join negotiations. The 400 lb van bomb, left outside the RUC station in Markethill, is thought to be the work of the republican splinter group, the Continuity Army Council. The IRA denied it was responsible. The Ulster Unionists called for Sinn Fein to be kicked out of the talks. The Continuity Army Council, which has never declared a cease-fire, is made up of former IRA members disaffected at Sinn Fein's dialogue with the British government. Mr. Trimble, who has fought a long battle behind the scenes to persuade his leadership colleagues to meet Sinn Fein in the talks, was furious. Ten minutes before the bomb exploded, his team had

made up its mind to attend Stormont Castle for a series of bilateral talks. The party immediately abandoned its plans.

I had not yet ruled on the eligibility of the DUP to request that Sinn Fein be expelled from the talks. That question became moot when the UUP now demanded that Sinn Fein be expelled. The UUP request had two bases: the *An Phoblacht* article and the Markethill bombing. The issue would now be squarely faced.

We worked all day and late into that night trying to get the process restarted, without success. A long series of private meetings yielded a determination to proceed, but no agreement on how to do so.

The negotiations resumed on September 23 to consider the UUP's demand for the expulsion of Sinn Fein. Trimble returned to the talks. He was careful to do so in the company of the loyalist party leaders. David Ervine of the PUP, Gary McMichael of the UDP, and their colleagues provided crucial political support for the UUP's reentry. They were associated with the loyalist paramilitary organizations—the men who had fought and died for the unionist cause; it was hard to accuse them of selling out the union. So for the first time Trimble and his delegates faced Adams and his delegates across the table. The two parties engaged in a tough, no-holds-barred debate. It was old, familiar rhetoric. The UUP alleged that the IRA and Sinn Fein were one. Sinn Fein denied it. But, in a real and important sense, it was new, because it was being done face to face, in the same room, across the table. The governments took the matter under advisement, and the meeting adjourned until the next day.

The governments spent most of the next day trying to decide how to handle the issue, so it was late in the day when the meeting resumed. To no one's surprise, the governments rejected the UUP's request that Sinn Fein be expelled from the talks. So long as the IRA was on cease-fire, Sinn Fein could remain. In a carefully worded statement, the governments reviewed the arguments that had been presented for and against the expulsion. They concluded that the language used by the IRA spokesperson in the *An Phoblacht* interview had been too vague and obscure to constitute a violation of the

Mitchell Principles, and that there was no evidence to link the IRA to the Markethill bombing.

The parties then approved the governments' motion on proceeding into substantive negotiations. Sinn Fein opposed the provisions on decommissioning, but they were outvoted by the other parties. On all of the other issues there was no disagreement.

It was with enormous relief that the officials of the two governments left Stormont late that night. At long last, fifteen months after the negotiations had begun, the way was open to substantive discussions. I was in the U.S. that week, so I missed the drama, though I received regular briefings by telephone. I was elated when I heard the results. Since the opening plenary session was supposed to conclude with a statement by the chairman, I had prepared remarks to be delivered at this point. Holkeri gave them to the parties for me.

I praised the participants for their perseverance, but acknowledged that greater difficulties lay ahead.

I told them that I understood the never-ending tensions between individual conscience and collective responsibility; between the demand of a constituency and those of the larger society; the simple, human conflict between duty to family and duty to public office.

For most human beings, I said, life is essentially an endless quest for respect—first, self-respect, and then the respect of others. There is no surer or more meaningful way to earn that respect than through service to other people. So I told them they would earn the respect of their fellow citizens, and their gratitude, when these negotiations were successfully concluded. And they would deserve it, because they would have done what no one had been able to do for so many years: bring lasting peace, political stability, and reconciliation to Northern Ireland.

I was elated for another reason. I was in the United States with Heather making final arrangements for the birth of our child. She was nearly due, and all was well. I promised her that, no matter what, I would make it home for the baby's birth. I returned to Northern Ireland in high spirits.

CHAPTER 13

Andrew's Peace

SUBSTANTIVE negotiations began in early October 1997 with a keen sense of anticipation among the participants. The negotiations were to be conducted in three strands. Strand One dealt with political arrangements within Northern Ireland; it was chaired by the British government, represented by Paul Murphy. Strand Two dealt with north-south relations; I chaired these talks, which were widely expected to be (and in the end were) the most difficult. Strand Three dealt with relations between the British and Irish governments and were conducted directly by them, although they kept the other participants informed of their discussions. This was the least difficult of the strands. London and Dublin had cooperated in organizing this process, and there was no doubt about their determination and ability to agree on Strand Three issues.

For the first few months, one day a week was set aside for each strand: One on Monday, Two on Tuesday, Three on Wednesday. So it was Tuesday, October 7, at 2:30 p.m., when I called the first Strand Two meeting to order. The comprehensive agenda on which the parties had agreed was extremely brief and vague; there were just general headings. That had made it possible to get agreement on the agenda; any attempt to be specific would have been impossible. I felt it important to get beyond the generalities, so I suggested that for the next five weeks the participants submit written statements of their positions on each of the five agenda items and then take one full day to discuss each. They agreed, and we scheduled a debate on the first agenda item ("Principles and Requirements") for the following Tuesday. I then invited each participant to give an opening statement. What followed shredded my optimism.

Although all of the parties were in the same room, the UUP refused to talk directly to Sinn Fein, communicating only through me. And when they spoke, the parties clashed sharply. It got so heated that, just prior to adjournment, I made an appeal to all of the participants to moderate their words. I told them that I was familiar with the tactic of demonizing one's enemy, having seen it at work in my own country in time of war. This process, however, was not about making war, but about ending war and establishing peace, political stability, and reconciliation. The more inflammatory the rhetoric, the more difficult the process would be. I urged them to be restrained outside of the talks and courteous inside. If they were, then perhaps we could reach agreement. We adjourned—and the parties immediately went out and repeated their statements to the press and public.

After discussing "Principles and Requirements," the participants dealt weekly with the remaining items on the comprehensive agenda. They were very general headings: "Constitutional Issues"; "Nature, Form and Extent of New Arrangements"; and "Rights and Safeguards." I was determined to keep my promise to Heather that I would be home for the birth. I talked with her by telephone at least once a day, so when I left Belfast on the afternoon of Tuesday, October 14, I knew that the time was near. I prayed that nothing would happen until I got there.

The timing turned out to be perfect. I arrived home late Tuesday night. On Wednesday, Heather began to experience contractions. Shortly after midnight, we went to the hospital. At 6:40 a.m. on Thursday, October 16, Andrew MacLachlan Mitchell was born. He weighed seven pounds fourteen ounces at birth. He was healthy. We were happy. Heather had some problems which required her to return to the hospital a few days later, and this delayed my return to Belfast, but it meant we were able to spend a few more days together.

Late in the middle of one night I sat watching Andrew sleeping. I began to imagine what his life would be like, lived, as it would be, almost entirely in the twenty-first century. I then started to think about how different his life would be had he been born a citizen of

Northern Ireland. I wondered how many babies had been born in Northern Ireland on October 16. What would *their* lives be like? How different would those lives be had they been born Americans? I picked up the telephone and called my staff in Belfast. After getting a routine briefing, I asked them to find out how many newborns had been delivered in the province on October 16. It didn't take long to get the answer: sixty-one.

For the next several days, the thought stayed with me. It was with me as I got up late on another night to comfort Andrew. Heather and I had such high hopes and dreams for our son. Surely the parents of those sixty-one babies had the same hopes and dreams. The aspirations of parents everywhere are the same: for their children to be healthy and happy, safe and secure, to get a good education and a good start in life, and to be able to go as high and as far as talent and willingness to work will take them. Shouldn't those sixty-one children in Northern Ireland have the same chance in life that we wanted for our son? Could they get it if Northern Ireland reverted to sectarian strife? There would always be the risk of babies being torn from their mothers' arms by the sudden blast of a bomb. When a mother sent her children off to school in the morning there would always be the nagging fear of random violence, the chance that she might never again see them alive. Why should people have to live like that? This conflict was made and sustained by men and women. It could be ended by men and women. And I knew those men and women. They were there, in Stormont. I had been with them for a year and a half, and I was now determined to stay with them to the end. I was also more determined than ever that these negotiations end with an agreement. For the sake of those sixty-one children, and thousands of others like them, we had to succeed. All of the doubts I had about my role in Northern Ireland vanished. No matter what, I would see it through, all the way to an agreement.

I felt an overpowering urge to touch my sleeping son. I picked him up and held him close for a long time. He couldn't hear me, but I told him that for him and for his sixty-one friends in Northern Ireland I was somehow going to get this job done, and when I did I would refer to it as Andrew's Peace.

By the time the opening stage of discussions was completed, on November 10, the parties were anxious for action. They had waited a long time to get into negotiations; the first few weeks had been discussions, not negotiations. So I set aside all of the following week for informal meetings among the chairmen, the governments, and the parties. I hoped—everyone hoped—that at last there would be some real give and take.

For most of the next two weeks there was an intensive round of private meetings. The UUP persisted in their refusal to meet with Sinn Fein, and Sinn Fein continued to insist on such a meeting. Notwithstanding that problem, there was a lot of activity. Holkeri, de Chastelain, and I met repeatedly with the governments and the parties; the parties held meetings among themselves, usually in bilateral form, and occasionally in groups of three or more. But, despite all of the activity, very little progress was made. The parties had submitted position papers on each subject. Now, at the meetings, they restated orally what they had submitted in writing. Although I tried, I was unable to get a genuine negotiation underway. Something else was needed to provide a spark—to generate some give and take.

There developed among all of the participants a consensus that a necessary next step was to prepare and agree on a document that would identify the key issues for resolution—essentially a more detailed comprehensive agenda. Only when all of the issues were seen together could the parties get a sense of where the necessary trade-offs and compromises might be made.

The schedule adopted at the beginning of the substantive negotiations provided that there would be periodic meetings in plenary session to review progress in the three strands and to receive reports from the two new subcommittees that had been established—the one on decommissioning and the one on confidence-building measures. A plenary meeting was held for that purpose on December 2. I had worked out in advance with all of the participants that the plenary would approve a change in the format of the meetings.

For the past year and a half, we had been gathering in a large room dominated by a large square table around which all the participants sat. Since there were now ten participants involved—two governments and eight political parties—and each had several delegates, there were often fifty or sixty people in the room. People were constantly coming and going, the party leaders were not always present, and it was often difficult to get consistency in the discussions. Microphones were needed, and the governments provided note-takers who faithfully prepared detailed minutes. The setting was not conducive to a candid exchange of views, let alone to hard bargaining.

A business committee had been set up to handle procedural matters, under the chairmanship of de Chastelain. The session had been held in a smaller room, without microphones, and was limited to two persons from each party. De Chastelain told me that the atmosphere had been good, that the informal setting, the smaller numbers, and the absence of note-takers had been helpful. He recommended that I try it for substantive negotiations, and I did. Without dissent the plenary agreed to my proposal to establish a working group which involved only the leader and deputy leader of each party.

We met the next day in a small room, without microphones or note-takers. I told those present that my objective was to reach agreement before the Christmas break on a detailed final agenda— a definition of the key issues and a mechanism to resolve those issues—so that when we returned in January we could proceed to the final phase of serious, substantive negotiations. We had two weeks to get this process moving.

There were meaningful, well-intentioned discussions. They are serious about words in Northern Ireland, and the words of agreement weren't yet there. There was a brief moment of optimism when the UUP and the SDLP appeared to reach consensus on a detailed final agenda. But Sinn Fein and the Irish government balked at some of the provisions, and the SDLP backed off, saying there had not been any agreement in the first place, just a discussion. The UUP was angry and upset. It was ironic, because the same thing had happened, in reverse, several times earlier in the talks—the SDLP believing it had consensus with the UUP, the latter on reflection asserting that the subject had been discussed but not agreed on. It pointed up the difficulty in a negotiation involving ten participants. Agreements, tentative or otherwise, tended to come unstuck when exposed to eight different political parties and two governments.

I found this failure especially hard to accept. There had been many setbacks before, but time was running out, and there was an unfortunate sense of failure developing—inside and outside the negotiations—a feeling that this process was doomed, that the conflict was impervious to solution. As ever, the specter of violence loomed over us. Beatings continued, and there were occasional killings—not enough to destroy the process, but enough to keep everyone on edge.

When the negotiators met on December 16, all of us were frustrated and deeply discouraged. Many were also angry, and that anger spilled out in the meeting. As is so often the case in Northern Ireland, it was a peripheral insult that triggered the outburst.

The rules of procedure provided that Strand Two meetings would be held in Belfast, London, and Dublin. All of the sessions so far had been held at Stormont, a suburb of Belfast. The nationalists wanted meetings in Dublin as a symbol of the all-Ireland dimension of the process. The unionists didn't like the idea, but agreed, with the condition that there would also be conferences in London, for precisely the opposite symbolic reasons. The governments had proposed meeting in London in January and Dublin in February. At an earlier business committee session there had apparently been agreement on the dates for these gatherings. Now, at the plenary, a nasty debate took place on whether there had in fact been an agreement in the business committee. Seamus Mallon of the SDLP was an important and influential figure in the talks. A member of Parliament, now the deputy first minister (designate) of the new Northern Ireland Assembly, he was liked and respected on all sides for his intelligence and integrity. He now said he had never, in all his years in Northern Ireland, seen such resentment, suspicion, and pain as he'd seen in the last few weeks. His words added to the somber mood. The higher the hopes, the greater the letdown. The discussion soon drifted into the underlying question of whether and when meetings should be held in Dublin and London. The UUP opposed moving the meetings at this stage in the process. Although the SDLP favored London and Dublin, it was opposed to holding sessions there until there was some progress in the talks; otherwise, they argued, going to the capitals would raise expectations, causing an even greater letdown. The governments, on the other hand, felt that a change of location might be a catalyst; they were so anxious for progress they were willing to try anything. The discussion then veered off onto leaks to the press and what the negotiators were saying about each other in public. Suddenly, we were back where we'd been for the previous, largely unproductive eighteen months: insult, invective, and recrimination.

Much has been said and written about my patience. I do have a lot of it, but I felt that I had just about used it up. Rarely in my life have I felt as frustrated and angry as I did on that day. We had been meeting for a year and a half. For hundreds and hundreds of hours I had listened to the same arguments, over and over again. Very little had been accomplished. It had taken two months to get an understanding on the rules to be followed once the negotiations began. Then it took another two months to get agreement on a preliminary agenda. Then we had tried for fourteen more months to get an accord on a detailed final agenda. We couldn't even get that, and we were about to adjourn for the Christmas break. Our failure, in the wake of expectations dramatically heightened by the events of the past few months, would be crushing. Yet here the delegates were, furiously debating what had or had not been agreed to in an earlier meeting about whether we should or should not move the whole process to London and Dublin, and who had said what to which newspaper.

I bit my lip, squirmed in my seat, and worked hard not to let my anger show. At that moment, I began to think about a deadline, earlier than the one at the end of May that Blair had already set. And it had to be a hard, unbreakable deadline. Already some British officials were saying privately that if we didn't finish by the end of May we could keep going as long as we were making progress. That would be unbearable, I thought. I couldn't stand the prospect of listening to this kind of talk for that long. Besides, and more importantly, without a hard deadline these people just would not decide anything: the decisions are so fraught with danger for them that they would just keep talking and talking and talking. Eventually, this process would just peter out or, more likely, some dramatic outside event—some new atrocity—would just blow it up. Either way, it would fail. It had to be brought to an end; that was the only possible way to get agreement. A deadline would not guarantee success, but the absence of a deadline would guarantee failure.

As we neared adjournment, I tried to steer the discussion back to what we had started the day with: the search for an understanding on a definition of the key issues and a mechanism to resolve those issues. But that discussion was listless and brief. This session was over. There would be no agreement on anything. The participants were sullen, with good reason. What hope could there be of concurrence on issues if they couldn't even agree on a description of those issues?

As each of the party leaders made closing comments, I debated with myself about what I should say. I was very angry, and I considered letting it all out. Perhaps an emotional outburst would shock them into action. But I decided against it. It was too late. Nothing I said now could produce an agreement. As bad as the situation was, I had to look to the future, to January, when we would return for the final effort. Once again, I would have to be upbeat. So I swallowed my disappointment and suppressed my doubts. Instead of criticism, I gave them what was as close as I ever got to a pep talk. I began by reminding them that this was the fifth and final time that there would be a lengthy break in the process; when we returned in January we would be in the final phase; there could be no further delay. I told them that I was deeply disappointed and frustrated, as I knew they all were. But, I reminded them, we had been disappointed and frustrated many times before. Each time, we had been able to keep the process moving forward. We had to do it again, one more time, one last time. The fact that we had come this far was a testament to their perseverance. I was convinced that they were serious about dealing with the difficult issues. But the real test would come when we returned in January. I repeated it again: There could be no further delay. They would have to make decisions about the future of Northern Ireland. They could not fail, because the alternative was unthinkable. I closed by asking them to make the next Christmas season one of peace, political stability, and reconciliation in Northern Ireland.

I don't know what effect it had on them, but it helped put me in the right frame of mind to go to the press conference that followed.

The governments had for a long time made it clear that they considered optimism to be an important part of my job description. Whenever there was a break in the process, or when total failure threatened, the British secretary of state for Northern Ireland and the Irish foreign minister asked me to hold a press conference to put the best face possible on events, to keep alive a sense of hope.

I shared their view of my role. I never made a false statement, but I worked hard to portray the situation as favorably as possible, to combat the widespread feeling that this process could not succeed. It was always a difficult balance, never more so than on this dark December day.

As always, the reporters were fair and courteous, but their skepticism was tangible. I couldn't blame them. For a year and a half they had heard my optimistic assessment of pessimistic events. They—especially those who lived in Northern Ireland—wanted the process to succeed. But they had an obligation to report the facts as they were, not as they wished them to be.

The news reports were as good as we could have hoped for under the circumstances. The *News Letter* reported that:

> Parties at Stormont broke for the Christmas holidays last night after failing to make headway on a key issues' agenda. They had no option but to agree to disagree and put their efforts on hold until they return on January 12. After many hours of fruitless attempts to make progress, talks chairman George Mitchell eventually emerged to confess that he was disappointed at the outcome.
>
> Mr. Mitchell told reporters: "While the inability to reach agreement is regrettable, the real question is whether they are prepared to deal with the issues in a serious way. I believe they are. I believe that the participants are committed to making progress. So I expect there to be substantive discussions when the talks resume on January 12 in Belfast."[1]

While I looked forward to spending Christmas with my wife, and the two-month-old son I had hardly seen, I was sad and discouraged on the flight home for the holiday.

CHAPTER 14

"I don't talk to murderers!"

OVER the Christmas break, the already bad political situation deteriorated sharply. At about 10:30 on the morning of Saturday, December 27, Billy Wright left his cell in the Maze prison, just outside of Belfast, for a visit with his girlfriend. He entered the back of a police van for the short drive to the prison visitors' center. As the van waited for the electronically controlled compound door to open, three other prisoners climbed over a ten-foot wall and across the roof of a nearby prison building. They jumped down from the roof, ran up to the van and opened the back door. At point-blank range they fired five shots into Wright's chest and back, killing him instantly. They also almost killed the peace process.

Wright had survived six previous assassination attempts. He was on the receiving end of so much murderous intent because he dished out even more himself. Known as "King Rat," a name he reportedly enjoyed, he headed the dissident Loyalist Volunteer Force (LVF), which opposed the peace process. Widely believed to have been involved in the murder of many Catholics, he was, at the time of his death, ironically, serving a prison term not for murder but for merely threatening to kill someone.

His killers were members of the Irish National Liberation Army (INLA), a republican splinter group which also opposed the peace process. Their reasons were the mirror image of those of the LVF. The LVF believed the peace process was a sellout of the union by the British government to republicans. The INLA felt the peace process was a sellout of a united Ireland by the Irish government (and the SDLP and Sinn Fein) to loyalists. In the twisted logic of the two competing groups, the only answer was violence—more war—until the other side capitulated totally.

The *Times* of London described the problem:

> Billy Wright is dead, but the Loyalist Volunteer Force will not die with him. With the two main loyalist paramilitary organizations observing the cease-fire, his dissident group will remain a magnet for Northern Ireland's plentiful supply of violent sectarian extremists who consider the Stormont peace talks a sellout. It has a clear and unchallenged niche in the market.
>
> Having successfully retaliated, the LVF may feel its honour is now satisfied, though it did warn ominously of "future attacks" yesterday. Since the peace process began in earnest, there have been several examples of loyalists and republicans staring into the abyss which they had inhabited for the previous quarter century and recoiling.
>
> The big danger is the perception that the Stormont peace talks are going nowhere, which plays into the hands of extremists on both sides. After three months the participating parties have yet to agree even on the issues to be resolved, and Unionists and Sinn Fein are still not talking to each other.[1]

The reaction to Wright's murder was predictable and immediate. Within hours, the LVF issued a chilling threat of retaliation. They said, in a written statement, "Billy Wright will not have died in vain. The LVF will widen its theatre of operations in the coming weeks and months." That day, some of their people riddled the entrance to a hotel in a Catholic area with gunfire, killing one man and wounding four others. Over the next few months, there was a rampage of sectarian murder across Northern Ireland. On New Year's Eve, thirty-one-year-old Edmund Treanor was gunned down in a bar. The LVF said that the killing was "in retaliation for the death of a true loyalist, Billy Wright" and warned, "This is not the end."[2] The next day, in retaliation, the INLA attacked a Protestant home in Newtown Butler. Nine shots were fired but no one was hit.

The secretary of state announced that British troops would return to the streets. They had been withdrawn six weeks earlier in an effort to build trust and confidence in both communities. The next day, 60 percent of the loyalist prisoners in the Maze prison voted to withhold their support for the peace process. This placed in jeopardy both the cease-fire of the main loyalist paramilitary organizations and the presence of the loyalist parties (the PUP and the UDP) in the talks.

Prisoners play an important role in the politics of Northern Ireland. They are seen by some in their communities as heroes who fought to defend a way of life and an oppressed people. Their views are of special significance to the political parties associated with paramilitary organizations—Sinn Fein on the nationalist side, the PUP and the UDP among the unionists. Even the constitutional parties recognize their role. This was demonstrated the next day when David Trimble, leader of the UUP, went to the Maze prison to try to persuade the prisoners to continue their support for the peace process.

In a front-page article, the *News Letter* summarized the deteriorating situation:

> The faltering peace process remained on a knife-edge last night after loyalist UDA and UFF prisoners refused to back their political representatives at the negotiating table.
>
> Amid fears that the three-year loyalist cease-fire is facing collapse, representatives of the Ulster Democratic Party failed to persuade their men inside the top security Maze to give the Stormont talks a fresh chance.
>
> Peace process negotiations are due to begin again in Belfast on Monday. Even though UDP leader Gary McMichael wants his team to return, the prisoners' refusal to pledge their support could have serious repercussions.
>
> He said: "Our position at the moment is quite precarious."
>
> Ministers in London and Dublin, also alarmed by the threat of more gun attacks on Roman Catholics by gunmen in revenge for the murder of LVF leader Billy Wright, are desperate to keep the peace process alive and the October 1994 loyalist cease-fire intact.[3]

As if to confirm the mood, on that day a five-hundred-pound bomb was discovered in a car in Banbridge. Fortunately the police were able to defuse the threat through a series of controlled explosions.

The situation was complicated by a growing chorus of demands by unionists for Mowlam's resignation. Ken Maginnis of the UUP, a leading member of his party's talks team, had been demanding her resignation for months. He was now joined by many others. Mo rejected the demands out of hand. To demonstrate her independence, she now took what was accurately described as the biggest gamble of her career. She went to the Maze prison to meet personally with the loyalist prisoners.

The spectacle was too much for many in Northern Ireland and across the United Kingdom: the secretary of state for Northern Ireland, one of the British government's highest-ranking officials, seeking a meeting with one hundred thirty men who had been convicted, by British courts, of murder, bombing, and other serious crimes.

> DUP security spokesman, Ian Paisley Jnr, said: "It was shameful that democracy and democratic politics has been undermined in an ego trip that has placed the prisoners centre on the agenda and abandoned the people of Northern Ireland."
>
> "It is clear that in the future the gangsters and the prisoners will have a greater say in the future of Northern Ireland."[4]

> Relatives of terrorist murder victims yesterday hit out at Ulster Secretary Mo Mowlam for visiting prisoners in the Maze.
>
> Women whose sons and husbands were innocent victims of terrorism said the Government was giving too much credence to men who brought heartache to thousands of families across the Province.[5]

But the headlines on the day after her visit told a different story: "She did it! Gamble pays off for 'Mighty Mo.' "[6] "Full credit to Mo Mowlam."[7] "Mowlam's Maze visit ensures talks will continue."[8] The prisoners agreed to continue their support for the talks, and the cease-fire by the main loyalist paramilitary organizations would remain intact. Praise and criticism of Mo aside, the fact remained that, with a combination of skill and daring, she had kept the process intact. (That didn't solve the problem posed by the LVF, of course, since it had split from the major paramilitary organizations and remained adamantly opposed to both the cease-fire and the peace process. As if to make that point clear, they immediately struck again. Terry Enwright, a twenty-eight-year-old Catholic father of two, was shot and killed as he stood outside the Belfast night club where he worked.)

Mo had done more than keep the talks alive. She and other British officials had worked with us and with the Irish government to come up with a document, entitled "Propositions on Heads of Agreement," to present to the parties. The prime ministers, Tony Blair and Bertie Ahern, had reviewed and approved the document. So when the talks resumed on January 12, it was not in a vacuum. Although the governments described it as "only the outline of an acceptable agreement," and although it was only two pages long, it was substantive and meaningful. It suggested, among other things, that there would be changes to the Irish Constitution and to British constitutional law; Northern Ireland would have self-governance through an Assembly elected by proportional representation; the existing Anglo-Irish Agreement would be replaced by a new one; new north-south institutions would be established; an Intergovernmental Council, involving members of Parliament from the Republic of Ireland, Britain, Northern Ireland, Scotland, and Wales, would be created; a Northern Ireland Bill of Rights would be adopted; and the contentious issues of decommissioning, security, policing, and prisoners would be addressed in ways not defined. Most of these "Heads of Agreement" found their way into the Good Friday Agreement. But that was still a long, hard way off.

Sinn Fein was the only party to oppose the proposal, which was approved by sufficient consensus. Sinn Fein didn't like the specificity of the language on the Northern Ireland Assembly. This was an "internal Northern Ireland solution," against which it had consistently argued. It did not recognize Northern Ireland as a separate legal entity; therefore, it opposed its having its own government. It was too early in the process for Sinn Fein to accept it, even though its leaders and everyone else knew that eventually a Northern Ireland Assembly would have to be included if there was to be an agreement.

Although the Irish government and the SDLP voted for the proposal, they were sensitive to the need to keep Sinn Fein in the process. So as soon as this document was approved, work began on a follow-up document which might be tilted slightly more to the nationalist side. That would offset what some saw as the unionist tilt of the "Heads of Agreement," because it included specific language on the Northern Ireland Assembly, which the unionists favored. In Northern Ireland, tit for tat is not limited to violent acts; it's necessary in the political process as well.

Despite the apparent progress, or perhaps because of it, the killings intensified. In Maghera, another Catholic, twenty-eight-year-old Fergal McCusker, was shot to death in the early morning hours by the LVF. As the participants began discussions in Strand One on the morning of Monday, January 19, they learned that Jim Guiney, a prominent thirty-eight-year-old loyalist leader with four children, had been killed by the INLA in a hail of bullets in Dunmurry. The response was swift and deadly. When the participants left the talks that same day they were told that a Catholic taxi driver, Larry Brennan, had just been shot to death in Belfast. This was the history of Northern Ireland in microcosm.

When the Strand Two meeting convened the next day, the delegates were somber. The escalating violence was clearly having an effect. There was a serious discussion, at the end of which the governments agreed to prepare a follow-up proposal. David Trimble had hailed the adoption of the "Heads of Agreement" proposal as a victory for unionism. It was apparent that the governments were going to try to even the score, to come up with a document that Gerry Adams could declare a victory for nationalism.

The talks struggled forward, and the sectarian murders continued. All of the deaths were tragic and senseless. But now a new and ominous development sent a shudder through the peace process.

The killers until then were thought to be members of dissident groups that had always rejected the cease-fires and the peace process: the INLA on the nationalist side and the LVF on the loyalist. The process had continued, with Sinn Fein and the loyalist parties in, because the main paramilitary organizations (the IRA, the UDA, and the UFF) maintained their cease-fires. Now it was publicly alleged that the UFF, the paramilitary organization associated with the Ulster Democratic Party, had been responsible for the killing of Larry Brennan. If that were so, the UDP was in violation of the Mitchell Principles and would have to be expelled from the talks. That could bring the peace process to an end.

The chief constable of the RUC, Ronnie Flanagan (who had succeeded Hugh Annesley), publicly charged that the UFF was indeed involved in some of the recent killings. That put the UDP, and its leader, Gary McMichael, on the spot. It also put the governments on the spot. They had worked hard, over a six-year period, to create an inclusive negotiation. If now, just as genuinely substantive discussions were beginning, the political parties associated with paramilitary organizations were thrown out, the whole strategy of the process would be undermined. On the other hand, the negotiations were firmly based on commitment and adherence to the Mitchell Principles of democracy and nonviolence. If those were now abandoned, the moral basis for the talks would disappear, and they would probably end in failure. It was an extremely difficult dilemma.

But the paramilitaries themselves made the result inevitable. On January 23, the UFF issued a written statement in which it admitted complicity in some of the killings. The document said that "The current phase of Republican aggression initiated by the INLA made a measured military response unavoidable. That response has concluded." The governments had no choice. They had to move to expel McMichael and his Ulster Democratic Party from the talks.

By an unfortunate coincidence, the talks were about to move to London. The long controversy over location had been settled: with much reluctance, the parties had agreed on London for the week of January 26, and Dublin for the week of February 16. When the decision was made, it was hoped that there would be some good news to announce in each of the capitals. Instead, it was the worst possible news. Serious discussion would be delayed; the talks would instead be devoted to the question of the expulsion of the UDP.

The Lancaster House is an elegant mansion in London regularly used by the government for important conferences. The stately meeting room, with high ceilings and ornately decorated walls, was a huge improvement over the drab office building in Stormont. As I walked up the grand staircase, I thought, Wouldn't it be nice if something good could happen here? But I knew that what was about to happen might mean the end of everything we had worked for.

It was supposed to be a Strand Two meeting. But I told the participants that before that meeting could take place a plenary session would have to be held to deal with the UDP issue. It was an awkward situation. The governments had the responsibility for deciding whether there should be an expulsion. In all of the previous cases, the request for expulsion had come from one party against another. In this case the governments initiated the request for expulsion. Mo Mowlam tried to walk a fine line, suggesting that the governments were raising the issue but hadn't yet made a final decision. But it was all too obvious. After lengthy discussions, the governments asked me to talk with McMichael and his colleagues. I agreed that they had to go; otherwise there would be no barrier between the talks and the violence on the streets. But I shared the view of both governments and several of the parties that McMichael and his colleagues were trying to keep the cease-fire intact. They were associated with the UFF, but they didn't control it. Better to get them back in after an appropriate interval so they could continue to speak out, within loyalist circles, for a continued (or resumed) cease-fire.

McMichael and about a half dozen of his colleagues were seated around a table in the small room that had been assigned to them. As I entered, their faces and gestures made clear that they knew why I had come. The conversation was short and to the point.

"The result is certain. You're going to be expelled."

"Yeah."

"Have you thought about leaving voluntarily?"

"Yeah. We're just talking about it now."

"Whatever you do, I hope you'll be able to say that you support the process and that you want to come back in as soon as possible. You guys have made a good contribution to this process."

"We're talking about all that now. We want to stay. It's others want us out."

They left that afternoon. They affirmed their support for the peace process and said they wanted to return as soon as possible.

The governments felt it necessary to complete the process and issue a formal ruling, even though there was no one left to expel. In their ruling they accepted the fact that the UDP sought to use its influence to oppose the violence of the UFF. But since there was no doubt in the governments' minds that there were close links between the UFF and the UDP, and the UFF had admitted its involvement in the murder, they had to conclude that there had been a clear breach of the UDP's commitment to the Mitchell Principles. The UDP was therefore no longer entitled to participate in the negotiations. But if over a period of weeks, a complete, unequivocal, and unqualified UFF cease-fire were demonstrated, and established through word and deed to have been fully and continuously observed, the governments would consider the possibility of the UDP rejoining the negotiations.[9] A month later, the UDP did come back.

The Strand Two talks resumed on Tuesday morning. The governments had promised to prepare and distribute a detailed paper on north-south institutions, but it wasn't ready. Each joint paper required extensive negotiations between the governments, acting on their own and as proxies for the two sides. The governments finally had the paper ready by that afternoon. It was entitled "Strand Two: North/South Structures," and consisted of six paragraphs and fourteen questions. I initiated a discussion in which all parties responded to the questions. We hoped that some common responses would emerge, on which we could begin to build an agreement.

During that discussion, Sinn Fein renewed its request for a meeting with the UUP. The parties still hadn't engaged, except around this table, communicating through me. The bitterness between them erupted in a profane outburst. Gerry Adams walked into the meeting room and told those present that he had approached the UUP's Ken Maginnis in the hallway outside and tried to speak with him. According to Adams, Maginnis replied: "I don't talk to fucking murderers," and walked away. The tension in the room was thick. It was relieved somewhat by Reg Empey, a thoughtful, moderate UUP delegate. He delivered an emotional explanation of the unionist position. The differences remained, but no one could doubt Empey's sincerity. His remarks appeared to make an impact on everyone, especially the nationalist delegates.

After another lengthy discussion on Wednesday, the Strand Two talks adjourned until February 10 in Belfast. The participants asked the chairmen to review the answers to questions given this week and prepare a new, composite document, identifying where there was common ground and where differences remained. It was slow going, but it was substantive discussion. Real issues were being debated.

That debate continued on February 10. It was sincere on all sides, and I began to hope that maybe this was leading somewhere. When we left the meeting that evening I thought, This is going well. It's about time for something bad to happen. And it did.

On January 29, the LVF issued a statement in which it said that it would end the killing of "innocent Catholics"; but it promised to carry on its campaign against "known republicans" and against "the Republicans of Ireland." The statement fueled the debate, which had begun as soon as the UDP left the talks in London, that a double standard was being applied—the unionists alleged that the IRA had been involved in the killing of some Protestants, so Sinn Fein should be expelled.

The LVF statement unleashed a new round of threats and counterthreats. The veteran correspondent David McKittrick described it with his usual insight in the *Irish Independent:*

Threats and counter-threats filled the air yesterday as the Loyalist Volunteer Force, which recently killed five Catholics, said it would wage "an unholy war against the nationalist community."

It was responding to a republican threat against the family of Billy Wright, the loyalist leader killed by the INLA just after Christmas.

The violence which left eight dead in December and January has left its mark. Last week an LVF statement that it was suspending attacks on "ordinary Catholics" was seen as progress of a sort, but yesterday's statement was full of renewed menace.

Security sources confirmed police had passed warnings of threats a week ago to the Wright family, who live in Portadown. Wright's father, David, who has made clear his opposition to violence and described killings in retaliation for his son's death as abhorrent, said the family was taking the matter seriously.

The LVF statement said: "If republicans do not come out and deny these claims . . . the LVF will take these threats seriously. If republicans do not come out and issue this statement of denial within the next 12 hours, the LVF will unleash an unholy war against the nationalist community. These type of sick threats against the late Billy Wright's family will not be tolerated."[10]

On February 9, Brendan Campbell was shot to death in Belfast. He was thirty years old and had a reputation for dealing in drugs. "Suspicion immediately fell on the group Direct Action Against Drugs—a group which RUC Chief Constable Ronnie Flanagan has described as 'a flag of convenience for the IRA.' "[11]

On the very next day, Robert Dougan,

a prominent loyalist with strong paramilitary connections, was killed as he sat in a car at lunchtime in one of Belfast's southern suburbs. Three men with IRA connections were later arrested.

The Ulster Unionist Party said it would demand Sinn Fein's expulsion if the Royal Ulster Constabulary confirmed the IRA's involvement, just as the loyalist Ulster Democratic Party had been ejected last month after its paramilitary wing . . . admitted killing three Catholics.

"If it is, as it presently looks, the work of the IRA then there's only one consequence," said David Trimble, the UUP leader.[12]

To blunt the unionist charges, the IRA issued a statement:

Contrary to speculation surrounding recent killings in Belfast, the IRA cessation of military operations remains intact. We reiterate our preparedness to facilitate a climate which enhances the search for a democratic settlement through real and inclusive negotiations.[13]

The statement only caused the unionists to step up their campaign for Sinn Fein's expulsion. The issue was effectively resolved by Flanagan, who told Mowlam that he believed the IRA had been involved in the Campbell and Dougan murders. Mowlam now had no choice.

The talks moved to Dublin. The meeting in London had been dominated by the expulsion of a unionist party. Now, by an odd coincidence, the conference in Dublin would be dominated by the expulsion of a nationalist party. Mowlam made a statement setting forth the case against Sinn Fein. This put the Irish government in a delicate position. Foreign Minister David Andrews made a careful statement in which he said "the IRA has a case to answer," but he also stressed the need to hear from Sinn Fein before a decision was made. The Sinn Fein delegates then began to pepper me with requests for adjournment and made other demands as well. I was informed by my staff that television and radio stations in Dublin were reporting that Sinn Fein was planning to take legal action to prevent its expulsion. I was careful not to give them any basis for action. The rules of procedure made it mandatory that I grant a party's request for an adjournment unless I felt that process was being abused. I granted three requests by Sinn Fein for adjournment. But I made it clear that I would not permit them to unreasonably delay the proceedings. The last adjournment took us into Monday evening. When we reconvened, Adams was absent. A member of my staff informed me that he was meeting with his attorneys, preparing for legal action.

As soon as I called the meeting to order, Martin McGuinness sought recognition. The Sinn Fein deputy leader has curly red hair, pale blue eyes, and a boyish smile. Unionists repeatedly charged that he was a top IRA official—some alleged he was the head of the IRA Army Council. But McGuinness steadfastly denied the allegations, and no formal charges had ever been brought against him. Like most of the other political leaders in Northern Ireland, he is an intelligent, forceful advocate for his party. I called on him.

"Mr. McGuinness."

"Mr. Chairman. We request an adjournment."

"What's the basis for the request?"

"We need more time to prepare for this meeting. An effort is going to be made to expel us. That's a serious matter. We need to prepare our response."

"You've known for a week that an effort was going to be made to expel you. It's been on television and in the newspapers all over Ireland and the United Kingdom. You've had plenty of time to prepare. Besides, I've already granted you three adjournments."

"It's a very serious matter. We didn't hear the secretary of state's statement until today. We need more time."

"Mr. McGuinness, it's my opinion that this request is solely for the purpose of delay. Under the rules I have the authority to deny a request for adjournment in such circumstances, and that's what I'm going to do. Your request is denied."

"Mr. Chairman, we demand an adjournment."

"Mr. McGuinness, that was the last word on the subject."

"Mr. Chairman—"

"When I said it was the last word, I meant it. Your request is denied. The meeting will proceed. The secretary of state is recognized to make a further statement on the matter."

Mowlam began to speak. I looked across the table at McGuinness. He was smiling at me. He had anticipated that his request would be denied. After Mowlam finished, there was a brief discussion. Then to minimize the risk that I might say or do something that their lawyers could use in the legal action they were obviously preparing, I adjourned the meeting briefly to write down my ruling on all of their requests. When we returned I made the ruling. I noted that Sinn Fein had made three requests: first, that I not convene a plenary on this issue; second, if a plenary were convened that it not be held immediately as they needed time to prepare their response; and third, that a stenographer be present to prepare a verbatim transcript of all discussions on this matter. I then pointed out that I had on that day, during the adjournments, met privately twice with the two governments, three times with Sinn Fein, and once with every other party.

I then explained why I considered it appropriate to call a plenary for the purpose of considering this matter. I gave Sinn Fein until 2:00 p.m. the next day to prepare its response, but I turned down the request for a stenographer. This meeting would be conducted as were all the others.

Sinn Fein brought its legal action the next day. As chairmen of the talks, Holkeri, de Chastelain, and I were among the named respondents. The Irish government provided us with counsel. The peace process was now moving from the negotiating table to the courts. As soon as I read Sinn Fein's petition, I knew its case was lacking in legal merit. The common law includes a principle which prohibits courts from deciding political questions. I wasn't familiar with Irish law, but I knew enough about the American version of the principle to be confident of my conclusion. If ever there was an issue that was a political question, it was this process of trying to negotiate peace in Northern Ireland. I told Mowlam and Andrews that I didn't think they should worry about an adverse decision. They felt the same way. But, wisely, they wanted a political agreement, not a legal victory. So they crafted a decision which expelled Sinn Fein but, subject to what happened in the interim, would let them back into the talks on March 9.

In their decision, the governments concluded that there was IRA involvement in the murders and that this constituted a clear infringement of the Mitchell Principles. They repeated their belief that the IRA is a group with a clear link to Sinn Fein. Therefore, the governments concluded, Sinn Fein should not be allowed to participate in the talks. But they went on to acknowledge the positive contribution that had been made to the peace process by the IRA cease-fire of August 1994 and its restoration in July 1997, and they also recognized the very significant and genuine efforts being made by Sinn Fein in working for peace. So if a complete, unqualified, and unequivocal IRA cease-fire was thereafter fully and continuously observed, Sinn Fein would be able to return.[14]

Although the decision was harshly criticized by some unionists, it was a pragmatic way to handle a difficult situation. Sinn Fein withdrew its legal action, and the process moved back to Belfast. But another week had been lost. And the negotiations grew increasingly vulnerable to outside violent actions. I expressed my growing concern at a press conference just before I left Dublin:

> I think it is becoming increasingly obvious that as the prospect of a successful conclusion of these negotiations improved, those who do not want to see a successful conclusion have taken more drastic and extreme measures. I'm concerned that violence from those groups opposed to the peace process may escalate as the negotiations move to the end game.

As I flew to the United States, I began to devise a specific plan to bring the talks to an early end.

CHAPTER 15

An Agreement at Last

DURING the next month, there were long, serious debates. Position papers were prepared, discussed, revised, and republished. All of the relevant issues were covered thoroughly, and then covered again. On Strand One, would there be a Northern Ireland Assembly? If so, how would its members be elected? Most importantly, how would it make decisions? The nationalists insisted on power-sharing, so the Assembly would need something like sufficient consensus to enact major legislation. In Strand Two, would there be new north-south institutions? If so, who would create them, the new Northern Ireland Assembly or the British and Irish Parliaments? The unionists, expecting to control the Assembly, wanted any north-south bodies to be created by and subordinate to it. The nationalists wanted such bodies to be established by the Parliaments and to be independent of the Assembly. As the debate ground on, I became more and more convinced that there had to be an early, hard deadline, in part because of the continuing violence and the constant threat of escalation.

Drawing on the experience of my six years as Senate majority leader and my three years in Northern Ireland, I reviewed in my mind the status of the negotiations, especially the crucial Strand Two talks, and tried to calculate how long it would take to bring about an agreement if we were under a hard and fast deadline. As I studied the calendar, Easter weekend leaped out at me. It had historical significance in Ireland. It was an important weekend in Northern Ireland, a religious society. If there were an agreement by

Easter there could be a referendum in late May and an assembly election in late June.

I knew that an agreement reached in the negotiations had to be approved in referendum by both the people of Northern Ireland and the people of the Republic of Ireland. Irish law requires a min imum of thirty days between the day on which a referendum ques- tion is published and the day on which the vote takes place. It was a foregone conclusion that an agreement would include the election of a new Northern Ireland Assembly, so that meant, in the British and Irish tradition, that there would have to be at least a month for the campaign to elect members of the Assembly. That required a mini- mum of two months after an agreement for final acceptance and an election. The governments were anxious that all of this take place before the peak of the marching season in early July. Obviously, then, we couldn't wait until the end of May; that would be too late.

I estimated that it would take two intense weeks to get it done. That meant we would have to start on March 30. I made up a day- by-day schedule for the two weeks from March 30 to Easter Sunday. Then, realizing that this would leave no margin for error, I decided to move the deadline up to midnight, Thursday, April 9. If we got to that time and hadn't quite finished we could go on into the Friday and Saturday of Easter weekend if necessary.

Once I had the plan clear in my mind, I discussed it with my staff, and with Holkeri and de Chastelain. I then talked with Mowlam, Murphy, and other British officials, and with Andrews, O'Donnell, Gallagher, and other Irish leaders. I met with Trimble and the UUP negotiating team and with Hume, Mallon, and the SDLP delegates. I did the same with all of the parties. I went around to all of them several times. Based on their comments, I re- vised some of the details—what we would do on each of the next fourteen days. But the deadline of midnight on Thursday, April 9, remained unchanged. By Tuesday, March 24, I was ready, as were all of the participants. I had spent weeks thinking about the plan and discussing it with them and working to get their support. Be- fore I presented the revised plan for their approval, I knew it would be agreed to unanimously.

I began the meeting that day by saying that every issue had been thoroughly analyzed and debated. The time for discussion was over.

It was now time for decision. I proposed that we meet continuously from Monday, March 30 through Thursday, April 9. For the first four days, we would solicit from the two governments and the eight political parties their final comments on the content of an agreement. On Friday, April 3, my two colleagues and I would present to them the first draft of a comprehensive accord. The parties would have overnight Friday to review it. We would then meet with each party for up to two hours on Saturday and Sunday to get their reactions to the first draft. Overnight Sunday we would prepare a second, final draft. That would be available to them on Monday, April 6. There would then be four days and nights of final negotiations, culminating in an agreement by midnight on April 9. I encouraged those delegates who did not live in the Belfast area to get hotel rooms nearby, so that everyone would be available at all times; the governments had offered to pay for their lodging, which was necessary and helpful.

There was no disagreement. The delegates were serious and determined. It wasn't clear that they could reach an understanding, because huge differences still existed among the parties on the key issues—the powers of the Assembly; how the north-south institutions were to be created, and what their powers would be; decommissioning of arms by the paramilitary organizations; and how many and how soon prisoners would be released. But I now felt certain that if this process failed it would not be because of a lack of effort and commitment by these participants. The next day, Wednesday, March 25, the independent chairmen issued a statement setting forth the schedule, which said in part,

> The participants know what needs to be done. It's now up to them to do it.
>
> We are totally committed to this effort. We are not considering any alternative plan in the event of failure because we believe that failure is unacceptable. These next few weeks will be decisive. Those who are determined to wreck the process cannot be allowed to prevail. The success of these negotiations will require steady nerves and courageous leadership by the men and women in whose hands rests the future of Northern Ireland. We believe they will be up to the challenge.

In the question-and-answer period that followed my reading of the statement at a press conference, I hammered home again and again the view that this was an absolute, inflexible deadline. I wanted there to be no doubt about that, in the minds of the media, in the minds of the public, and, most importantly, in the minds of the participants.

> MEDIA: Senator Mitchell, effectively what you are saying is the next fifteen days are make or break for this process, is that correct?
> SENATOR MITCHELL: Yes. . . . As far as I am concerned, there is a deadline and we can meet that deadline. This is not a matter of time. We have been at this for two years; it could be discussed for another two years or for another twenty years. It isn't that there hasn't been enough time for discussion, it is that there has not been a decision required and the only way to bring this to a conclusion is to require a decision. I believe the time for that is now.[1]

The headlines and stories the next day said that I'd imposed a deadline. But the reality was that I didn't impose anything on the participants. I didn't have to. They accepted the deadline because they were as eager as I was to get an agreement. It was that attitude, more than anything else, which gave me hope. The high stakes involved were clear. The *Irish News* described them in an article, under the headline "Bloodshed Looms If Parties Fail To Settle."

Those who opposed the peace process kept up their deadly assault, and there was another eruption of violence over the weekend. An incident of a different kind also created problems. Someone inside the British government leaked to the press an internal memorandum by Mo Mowlam's new press secretary. In it he proposed that the government plan a media campaign to gain public support for any agreement that might result from the negotiations. Among other things, he wrote:

> We are embarking on what in effect will be the most crucial election campaign in Northern Ireland's history. During the

next 10 weeks we need to convince the Northern Ireland public both of the importance of what is at stake, and also convince
them that not only is agreement possible, but they have a vital
role to play in endorsing it.

. . . [T]hat will require a sustained, committed and coherent
effort right across government. The message needs to be rein-
forced on every conceivable opportunity and the benefits of an
agreement underlined in every possible way. The Northern
Ireland public needs to be in no doubt about how a deal will
improve every aspect of their quality of life. We need to con-
vey that message. That means a concerted effort by all ministers and departments in every speech, interview and meeting.[2]

I thought the memorandum was rather unremarkable, and what one
would expect in such circumstances. But it drew heavy criticism
from unionists. That made the Ulster Unionists uneasy, and anything that made them anxious was a threat to the process.

This was the latest in a long series of leaks from within the British
government, going back to the very beginning of the negotiations.
Leaks were to be expected. But those from the Northern Ireland
Office were different: they had the apparent intent to undermine
the peace process, even though the government itself was an architect of that process. They also seemed to be intended to embarrass
Mo Mowlam. Several of them were timed to cause her maximum
difficulty.

While the talks were in session there were daily—sometimes several times a day—meetings in the secretary of state's office. The participants were the British government, the Irish government, the
independent chairmen, and all of their staffs—as many as twenty-
five or thirty people in the room. For the British, Mowlam and
Murphy were usually there, with their personal assistants. There
also were several career civil servants from the Northern Ireland
Office—the political director, the security chief, the director of public information. For the Irish, Andrews, O'Donnell, and Gallagher
were there, with their assistants and civil servants and security offi-
cers. I often looked around the room, wondering if one of those
present—all trusted aides to senior government officials—was the

leaker. The leaks became so common that we joked about them. "How long will this take to be leaked to the press?" I often asked after making a recommendation on a course of action, or a decision on how to proceed that day. "If you leak this, leak it accurately," was a frequent addition to a statement. Such remarks were usually greeted with nervous laughter. But the truth was we didn't know who was doing the leaking, and it continued almost to the very end of the process. The situation was difficult for Mo, but she did the only sensible thing she could do—shrug it off and move forward.

For five days we met almost nonstop with the parties, trying to draw out of them possible areas of compromise. I was determined to get to the first landmark in the schedule: an initial draft of a comprehensive agreement by Friday, April 3. We had more than enough paper—over the preceding weeks the governments and the parties had submitted dozens of position papers on every issue. The hard part was putting them together in a way that would be acceptable to parties with sharply different objectives. The unionists wanted a continuation of the union—Northern Ireland as part of the United Kingdom—and a strong, majority-run Northern Ireland Assembly; they desired only minimal north-south institutions, with power derived from the Assembly, not independent of it. The nationalists wanted just the opposite: a united Ireland, north and south joined together in a single sovereign state; short of that, they looked for an Assembly in Northern Ireland in which power would be shared by the Protestant majority and the Catholic minority; and they wanted strong north-south institutions created directly by the British and Irish Parliaments and therefore independent of the Northern Ireland Assembly. Each side was deeply suspicious of the other, with a presumption of bad faith. Still, with all of these serious differences, in this tense atmosphere, against a background of continuing violence, I was convinced that an overall compromise was possible.

On the overriding issue—the union or a united Ireland—the unionists clearly would prevail; that was widely accepted. On the Assembly, I was confident that Sinn Fein eventually would accept and participate in such a body, and that the unionists would agree to power-sharing. They had done as much in these negotiations; the voting procedure that we used—we called it sufficient consensus—was a form of power-sharing. If we could get an agreement here, it would help to persuade the unionists that the concept was workable. The moment of truth would come over the north-south institutions. We would have to be innovative to reconcile the differences on this highly emotional issue.

Some problems we would not be able to resolve directly. The criminal justice system and the police were extremely controversial. Nationalists were harshly critical of them; unionists strongly defended them. We would have to establish commissions—experts who would have time and perspective—to study and report the following year.

The first week was moderately productive. In addition to position papers on specific issues, I asked the governments to give us their best estimate of possible areas of agreement. Civil servants, many of them lawyers, worked tirelessly through the week to come up with these drafts, which formed the basis of the agreement that was eventually reached. On the British side, among those involved were Quentin Thomas, David Hill, and Stephen Leach; on the Irish side were Dermot Gallagher, Tim Dalton, David Donoghue, David Cooney, and others. Although most of the press and public attention focused on the political leaders, these men, and other men and women like them, made invaluable contributions to the process.

Over the nearly two years of negotiations, I had on many occasions invited Hill and Cooney into my office for private discussions. They are both skillful civil servants, around forty years old, who have been involved in Northern Ireland on behalf of their governments for many years. They have the even temperament and good judgment that inspire confidence. Frequently, the governments disagreed over issues or procedures and struggled to resolve their differences. Since the cooperative effort by London and Dublin was the foundation upon which the entire peace process was built, I felt it crucial that their cooperation continue, and regarded it as an important part of my job to facilitate that cooperation. Without compromising their governments, Hill and Cooney were able to give me a better understanding of the issues and help guide me toward their solution. They were truly unsung heroes of the peace process.

We reviewed the drafts provided by the governments and the proposals, written and oral, from the parties. We were able to put together drafts on all of the relevant issues, except for those involved in Strands One and Two. Those were, of course, the most important. And they were the same questions we had been wrestling with for months: the Assembly—how its members would be chosen and how it would make decisions; and the north-south institutions—how they would be created, how many of them there would be, and what their relation would be to the Assembly. Since there were still deep differences over many issues in those strands, and since this was just the first draft, we decided to include options on several key issues. Then, after we got the parties' reactions over the weekend, we would choose among the options and come up with a definitive text for the final draft on Monday. Since I was concerned that this document would be leaked to the press, the presence of options—something less than final language on key issues—would emphasize its nature as a draft, and therefore have less impact when leaked.

We worked very late Thursday night and all day Friday getting the document ready. Holkeri, de Chastelain, and I, and our staffs—Martha Pope, David Pozorski, and Kelly Currie from the United States, Clifford Garrard from Canada, and Marcus Laurent from Finland—gathered around a small conference table in my office. The basic document we worked off was a draft submitted jointly by the governments. It covered all of the issues other than those in Strands One and Two. The governments had yet to agree on those two critical subjects, but on most of the others—changes in the Irish Constitution and in British constitutional law, prisoners, policing, criminal justice, a new British-Irish Council—they had worked out a common position. We compared their joint position with those which had been submitted by the parties and made changes that we thought would enhance the prospect of agreement. Although there were many issues and dozens of papers, we were able to proceed fairly rapidly because we had read all of the papers many times and heard them discussed over hundreds of hours. Among ourselves there were no differences on issues.

On Strands One and Two, we did not make definitive choices in this draft. We listed the principal options on each key question and invited the parties to give us their final views on those issues over the weekend. I knew that every participant would find some parts of this document difficult to accept. So I wrote a covering memorandum emphasizing that it was just a draft, highlighting the various options contained in the sections on Strands One and Two, and restating our intention to meet with all of the parties over the weekend; we distributed a schedule of those meetings, which would run from Saturday morning through Sunday afternoon. That left us Sunday evening and night to prepare the final draft.

I was confident of our ability to get the draft out on Friday evening. This was a critical step in the process. For the first time the participants would see all of the issues laid out in a single document. They could evaluate the trade-offs involved and determine whether they, and their constituents, could accept them. When I devised the schedule for this last phase of the negotiations, I regarded the two-draft process as essential to eventual success. There had to be the opportunity for the negotiators to react to the first document, to let off steam, then hopefully move on to the final draft. So my disappointment was deep when I learned on Friday evening that we would not be able to produce the first draft on schedule.

There was enormous media attention focused on the talks at Stormont, and it intensified dramatically during this last phase. But on Wednesday of this week, even more attention was focused on 10 Downing Street, the prime minister's office in London. Bertie Ahern flew from Dublin to London to meet with Tony Blair. The stakes were high. In an insightful editorial, the *Financial Times* on April 3 summarized the problems, and the potential, confronting the prime ministers.

> The emergence of what Bertie Ahern, the Irish prime minister, calls "large disagreements" between himself and Tony Blair sounds very worrying, with only a week to go till the deadline both governments had set for agreement on Northern Ireland's future at the multi-party talks in Belfast. But in fact it may be a sign that the talks, and the deadline, are at least being taken seriously by all the parties involved.
>
> Until a week or so ago, talk of an agreement being "agonizingly close" came mainly from the two governments, and from moderate Northern Irish parties such as the Catholic SDLP and the small, bicommunal Alliance. Both Sinn Fein, the polit-

ical wing of the IRA, and more crucially the Ulster Unionists, were making skeptical noises.

But now Sinn Fein is signaling its eagerness to be in on the deal: and yesterday David Trimble, the Unionist leader, voiced his concern that Irish "posturing" might harm the talks.

"It may push back the date for agreement," he said, "and that would be cruel to the people of Northern Ireland who have a certain hope."

That statement is significant. If Mr. Trimble thinks the Irish government is posturing, he must believe, on the basis of several long meetings he has had with Mr. Ahern in the last few months, that its real position is one he could accept. Implicitly, at least, he is saying he now believes an agreement really could be reached next week, if only Mr. Ahern plays it straight.

For years a constitutional settlement in Northern Ireland has been a hypothesis with which all sides could play. Now suddenly it seems an imminent reality, and both sides are working frantically to ensure it does not take a form which will be hard for them to sell to their supporters.

The sticking point is the proposed north-south bodies. Mr. Ahern is trying to hold Mr. Blair to the concession made by his predecessor, John Major, who agreed that these bodies should be set up by legislation. Mr. Blair can counter by pointing to another clause in the 1996 Frameworks Document, which said their functions should be defined with the agreement of the parties.

It should not matter. Legislation should hold no terrors for unionists, provided it is clear that the bodies will act only by consensus, and that their northern members will be answerable to the new Northern Ireland Assembly. But equally the Irish government should recognise that accepting such bodies at all is a very bold step forward by the unionist side, and should not jeopardize this by insisting on a symbolic point that is hard for unionists to swallow.

The prize is within reach. We may be about to witness the most exciting, and most hopeful moment in Irish history since the island was partitioned in 1921.

The Blair-Ahern negotiations highlighted the importance—and the difficulty—of the issues in Strand Two. The *Irish Times* accurately described the problem on April 2:

> The Taoiseach and the British Prime Minister were locked in crucial negotiations late last night in a determined bid to overcome "large disagreements" between the two governments over the terms for a political settlement on Northern Ireland.
>
> With the deadline for agreement just one week away, Mr. Ahern and Mr. Blair were under pressure to narrow their differences and agree a common position as Senator George Mitchell prepared to present a draft agreement to the participants in the multi-party talks tomorrow.
>
> But the scale of the task—and the possibility of failure—was dramatically underlined by Mr. Ahern as he left Dublin for the Downing Street summit. Signaling a night of tough talking and hard bargaining, Mr. Ahern said that there were "large disagreements" which could not be "cloaked." He added ominously: "I don't know whether we can surmount this."
>
> . . . Unionist sources last night said that the document presented to Mr. Trimble by Mr. Blair at Chequers last Sunday was not a British response to an Irish draft apparently submitted to London two weeks ago. Describing the paper as a "summary" of the options, the sources confirmed that they had "very real" difficulties in agreeing with Mr. Blair the status of the North-South Council and the "source of its authority."

The last paragraph in the *Irish Times* story captured a serious complication in the situation. The parties were negotiating at Stormont. The prime ministers were negotiating in London, but they were in contact with some of the parties at Stormont: the British with the UUP, the Irish with the SDLP and Sinn Fein. For a few days, the other parties—and the independent chairmen—were not directly in the London loop. We received periodic reports, but they were often outdated, having been overtaken by events. The other parties grew increasingly frustrated and resentful. Several of them came to me to request that I call the prime ministers and ask them to come to Stormont and combine the two sets of negotiations into one. I declined. I told them that while I felt it important that the prime ministers come to Stormont, it was too early. Their impact would be huge for a few hours, at most a few days; it was better that they arrive at the very end. As to their negotiations in London, I hoped that they could come up with an acceptable agreement. Since Blair was keeping Trimble advised, and Ahern was doing the same for Hume and Adams, that was a reasonable expectation.

Late on Friday afternoon I notified all of the parties that they could expect the first draft that evening, hopefully by nine o'clock. At 6:30, I received a telephone call from Blair and Ahern.

"Hello."

"Hello, George. This is Tony Blair. Bertie's on the line with me."

"Hello, Prime Minister. Hello, Taoiseach."

"George, we know you're planning to deliver the first draft of the agreement to the parties tonight."

"That's right. I told them a little while ago that we'd try to get it to them by nine o'clock."

"You're aware that we've been talking here about Strand Two issues."

"Yes, I know. How's it going?"

"Well, we're making good progress but we're not quite finished. That's what we're calling about."

I started getting edgy. "What do you mean?"

"We aren't finished on Strand Two issues yet so we don't think you should include a Strand Two section in the draft you give them tonight."

"How can I do that?"

"Well, perhaps you could give them a draft on everything else and just provide an oral summary on Strand Two. Just talk about it, but don't give them anything on it in writing."

I was stunned. There was a long pause as I tried to figure out what to say. Ahern jumped in.

"George, this is Bertie. We know this makes it difficult for you. But we're making progress here. We're close to an agreement. We just need a little more time to get there."

"How much more time?"

"I'm not sure. The weekend should be enough."

"Well, this creates a real problem here. Getting a first draft to them tonight was an important part of my deadline strategy. I don't know how to handle this. But, look, we're here serving at your request and we've always cooperated with you before and we'll try to do so now. I'm just not sure how to proceed. Let me give it some thought. I want to talk to John and Harri and the party leaders. I'll call you back after that."

"That's fine."

"That's all right."

"OK. It'll probably take me a while to get through the process of consulting everyone, but I'll get back to you tonight."

I hung up the phone and sat there staring at it for a few minutes, trying to decide what to do. I genuinely liked and admired both Blair and Ahern. They were working very hard, taking huge risks. I would do just about anything for them. But what they wanted would badly disrupt the schedule I had worked so hard to put together; it could mean failure to make the deadline. Somehow I had to figure out a way to accommodate their request and still keep the process on track.

I called together Holkeri and de Chastelain, our staffs, and the British and Irish officials who were at Stormont. I related to them my conversation with the prime ministers. They all were deeply disappointed. Holkeri, de Chastelain, and I then started a round of consultation with those party leaders who were at Stormont. They weren't all there, but those we saw, one party at a time, were unanimous and emphatic. They did not want to receive a partial document. The whole point of the initial draft was to have, for the first time, a comprehensive paper. Given the importance of Strand Two, a draft that didn't include those issues would be incomplete. This was the wrong way to proceed. Better to delay than to do it wrong, even though a delay could have serious adverse consequences.

Gary McMichael was especially emphatic. His father, a prominent unionist, had been shot to death during the Troubles. Now Gary, not yet thirty years old, was thrust into political leadership. I liked Gary and had gotten along well with him from the beginning; we had never exchanged a harsh word. He wasn't harsh now, but he was very blunt and, for him, emotional.

"Senator, we agreed a process. We want to stick to that process. We don't want a partial document."

"Even if it's got everything in it except one section?"

"If it doesn't have Strand Two it's not complete. We don't want anything other than a complete document."

Gary usually spoke fast, with a distinct Belfast accent, so at times I didn't catch every word. But he was talking slowly and clearly now, for emphasis. I understood every word; and I appreciated the passion behind the words.

After these meetings, as much as I wanted to proceed, I knew I could not. The prime ministers had asked me to go forward, but their principal concern was that I not go forward on Strand Two. The prime ministers can live with a delay, I thought, since their principal concern—nothing in writing on Strand Two—would be met. Holkeri, de Chastelain, and our staff all agreed.

I called Blair and Ahern and told them of my decision. As I expected, they had no objection. I said that I had to have the product of their negotiations by Sunday evening. We were going to miss the first landmark, a first draft by Friday. That would make it difficult to reach the Thursday deadline. If we missed the second landmark, a final draft by Monday, there could be no hope of getting agreement by the deadline. They assured me they would forward a Strand Two paper to me by Sunday evening.

We then met again with the British and Irish ministers and their staffs to consider how to handle this with the parties and the press. The governments' officials were in conflict: they were upset at their prime ministers for having taken over the negotiations without coming to Stormont. But they also were worried that Blair and Ahern might be blamed for the delay—the consequences of which no one could foresee. In the tension of the moment, there was the constant fear that the process might at any time collapse into failure. In not very subtle language, they asked that the independent chairmen assume responsibility for the delay, or at least make the explanation so vague that no blame could be assigned. We agreed. We understood that absorbing blame was one of the reasons we were there. Besides, we knew that Blair and Ahern were working hard, at considerable political risk, to bring this process to a successful conclusion. If they could give us on Sunday evening an agreement on Strand Two issues that was acceptable to the parties, it would be more than worth the delay.

We then met with the parties. They were serious and concerned but understanding and agreeable, especially since the decision to delay had been at their urging. We told them that we were going to hold a press conference, briefed them on what we were going to say, and asked them to be supportive in their statements.

The press contingent was much larger than we had been accustomed to. I said we had spent the past several days holding dozens of meetings, covering hundreds of hours, talking with all of the participants in an effort to prepare a comprehensive document covering all of the issues, but that we were not able to get the full document ready as we had hoped by that evening. I hoped to be able to have the full document ready in the next few days.

Then the questions began. I tried to honor the governments' request and also to be fully responsive and accurate in my answers. It wasn't easy. For example:

MEDIA: Senator Mitchell, how helpful would it have been to your efforts tonight if the two governments had been able to agree in London?

SENATOR MITCHELL: I think the prime ministers and the government officials deserve a lot of credit for the tremendous effort, energy, and concentration that they put into this. They've made an invaluable contribution to the entire process. The governments of course are the organizers and sponsors of this entire negotiating effort. Obviously the more people agree on the more issues the better off we are, and we are encouraging everyone to proceed in discussions across a wide range of issues and involving many parties that will ultimately help us move forward. So I think common sense indicates that the earlier anyone can agree on any aspect of these issues the better off, and I'm confident that will happen.

MEDIA: Senator, what held up the agreement today?

SENATOR MITCHELL: . . . It was simply that we were not able, we the chairmen, were not able to get it ready in time, given the very large number of issues, the number of parties—we're dealing here with ten different entities—and the, simply the capacity, to go through them all and have a document ready.

MEDIA: To what extent did what happened in London, and

your conversations with Mr. Blair and Mr. Ahern, what extent did that change your ability to complete the comprehensive document tonight?

SENATOR MITCHELL: Well, I talk to Mr. Blair and Mr. Ahern often on many occasions and on many issues. I said earlier I applaud them for the tremendous effort and energy that they've put into this process. We have also talked to a large number of other participants and obviously, as I answered to the question over here, it would have been helpful had they been further along. But that's true of many other issues and many other parties and it's true of us as well.

MEDIA: Did they ask you not to forward the comprehensive document tonight, did they make it clear to you that they would prefer that you did not forward that document tonight?

SENATOR MITCHELL: No. That assertion is incorrect.[3]

That last answer was troubling. The prime ministers did not ask me not to forward the comprehensive document tonight; to the contrary, they wanted me to present it to the parties, but without the Strand Two section. That request had caused the delay. So my answer was technically true, given the way the question was asked, but it was not fully responsive. I had worked hard for three years to be truthful and cooperative in my dealings with the governments, the parties, and the press. To my knowledge, I had not misled anyone during that time. I had, of course, repeatedly been optimistic when things weren't going well, and I had frequently interpreted events in a favorable way. But none of that had been misleading. This answer was, and it worried me. I resolved not to let it happen again.

It wasn't just the press conference: of greater concern was the fate of the process. I prayed that Blair and Ahern would come up with something that everyone could live with. That would be a huge step forward. The press reports the next morning were as good as we could have hoped for. Under the headline "Mitchell fails to come up with draft," the *News Letter* wrote:

Talks chairman, former Senator George Mitchell, had hoped to present the parties with a draft settlement for a weekend of intensive discussions, but he was not able to complete the draft by last night's deadline.

The delay was described by the parties as a disappointment but all vowed to continue attempts to secure peace in the coming week.[4]

The headline in the *Irish News* was "Setback as Mitchell delays key document." The story began:

The multi-party talks suffered a serious setback late last night when chairman Senator George Mitchell was unable to table a comprehensive document giving the outline for a possible peace settlement.

Originally Senator Mitchell was to have met the parties at 8pm—but it was not until 9:40pm that he called the leaders of the UUP, SDLP, Sinn Fein, Alliance, UDP, PUP, Women's Coalition and Labour to a top floor conference room at Castle Buildings.

This followed consultations with some parties during which Senator Mitchell is said to have explained that only one part of the paper was ready to be tabled.[5]

We had planned a weekend of intense activity. It turned out to be active, but at first it was not intense. We met with the parties, continued to edit and revise the draft, and anxiously awaited news from London. Toward the end of the weekend things got very taut. Blair and Ahern had reached agreement. Their officials brought a document to my office on Sunday evening. Of the many meetings we had with government officials in the nearly two years of negotiations, this was the most difficult. The political officials were not there. But high-level civil servants, whom we knew well and liked, were. As I read the document I knew instantly that it would not be acceptable to the unionists. I didn't know what communication there had been between Blair and Trimble, but I knew that Trimble would never, could never, accept this. It was precise on the independent authority of the so-called "cross-border bodies" that were to be set up to implement the decisions of the new North/South Ministerial Council;

in addition it referred to annexes that would detail the potential areas of north-south cooperation. We didn't have the annexes, as they were still in the process of being prepared; but any listing of specific areas of cooperation would be red flags to the unionists.

That was troubling. To add to my already high anxiety, the government officials now requested on behalf of the prime ministers that we include in our comprehensive document what they had agreed on *without any changes*. They did not want a single word or a single comma altered. And we were told it should go in as *our* draft, not theirs. As one British official delicately put it:

"We think the whole document should be yours, not just parts of it."

"But," I protested, "the rest of it is ours. Even though the parties and your people drafted it, we made changes wherever we wanted. This is different. Here you're asking us not to change it but to still call it ours."

"We think that's the best way to proceed," replied one embarrassed Irish official.

This was unlike the process we had followed on all of the other sections of the comprehensive document, and it was very difficult to accept. I looked at my colleagues. Harri's jaw was tight; John's face was flushed. I could tell, without a word being said, that they were upset.

I thought briefly about adjourning the meeting and demanding that their political superiors be brought in. But that would have undercut those present, and lost valuable time. We had to get the draft ready for distribution tomorrow to have any chance of meeting the Thursday deadline. We had to resolve this, here and now.

As we talked, gradually it became clear that there were differences between the governments. The Irish were much more insistent that the document not be changed. By their words, tone, and body language, the British made it clear that they were less firm. They were going along with the demand for the sake of governmental unity, it seemed to me, but if we wanted to make a change, they wouldn't protest. That confirmed my initial assessment of their agreement. The SDLP and Sinn Fein would like it, so the Irish wanted it unamended. The UUP would not like it, so the British hoped it would be changed.

On the other hand, the British were unyielding that whatever we put in on Strand Two be identified as our proposal, not that of the governments, even though everyone in the United Kingdom and Ireland knew by now that Blair and Ahern had been negotiating on Strand Two issues. That also confirmed my initial assessment.

After hearing them out, we requested that my two colleagues and I and our staff have a chance to consider their demands and decide what to do. We were all deeply concerned. This was so unlike anything we had ever before been asked to do that we had no context or precedent to guide us. De Chastelain reviewed the circumstances and suggested that we had essentially three options: we could accede to their demand; we could include their Strand Two document within our comprehensive draft but identify it as theirs, not ours; or we could rewrite it and then include it as ours, as it would then be.

We quickly ruled out the third option. It was by now early Monday morning. We had to get the full draft out that day, preferably by late afternoon. In order to accomplish a meaningful rewrite of the Strand Two section, we would have to show it to all of the parties and give them time to do their internal consultation and respond to us; then we would have to rewrite it, taking their views into account. That would take days, not hours. By then the notion of a Thursday deadline would have been destroyed. A rewrite was out of the question.

We then considered the second option, which was to do half of what they demanded: include their proposal, without change, which they wanted, but identify it as theirs, which they didn't want. We drafted and redrafted language to make the identification, trying to compose it in a way that would be accurate but not harmful to the governments. We couldn't find the words. We let off steam among ourselves as we considered our unusual situation. But we never lost sight of the fact that this whole process was organized and sustained by the governments, who were working hard to achieve agreement under extremely difficult, even dangerous circumstances; whatever our discomfort, we were not at political risk, as they were. Grudgingly, and with much difficulty, we gave up on the second option.

That left acceding to their demands, which in the end we did. We were influenced by the fact that the British were in a perilous situation, and by the fear that if the governments split over this issue, there wasn't enough time both to mend the split and make the deadline. It was imperative that they stay united and that we all mount the last drive for agreement together, even though the route they had chosen disquieted us.

It was Monday morning when we notified the British and Irish of our decision. I went back to the hotel for a few hours of sleep. I consoled myself with the thought that we might be able to get the document to the parties before our target of six o'clock that evening. That would give us, and the process, a little more time to absorb the tremendous negative reaction that would come from the parties. I was certain that, in the tradition of Northern Ireland politics, they would accept without comment everything in the agreement they liked but would complain loudly about anything they didn't like. I had originally hoped for a whole weekend for them to vent, then four full days to recover and agree; now there would be Tuesday to complain and then only two days to recover and agree. It was getting more and more problematic.

When I returned to Stormont on Monday, I was jolted by the news that the annexes to the governments' Strand Two paper still had not been negotiated. These were not simple, noncontroversial issues. The annexes were supposed to be lists of possible areas of cooperation, in various categories of importance and certainty—one annex listed subjects on which the governments were committed to cooperation while another contained subjects on which they would consider cooperation. When we had received their document the previous evening I thought it was nearly complete. I now learned it was not.

That forced another uncomfortable decision on us. We could distribute the document without the annexes, but that would make it incomplete—something the parties had told us emphatically they didn't want. Or we could wait until the governments fully negotiated the annexes. That seemed to make the most sense under the circumstances, especially since I hoped they might be able to get it done in time for us to meet our target.

We were confident that once we got Strand Two settled, there would be no difficulty with Strand One. Of course the corollary was that every delay in settling Strand Two also delayed Strand One. It was widely accepted that, ultimately, the two major parties, the UUP and the SDLP, each the largest in its community, would have to negotiate the Strand One issues directly. On Saturday evening, I had convened a meeting of the two parties in my office, during which it became apparent that the Ulster Unionists would not be ready to conclude on Strand One until agreement was reached on Strand Two. After a two-hour discussion I formed the opinion that it would take the two parties a day at most to settle all of the Strand One issues. But until Strand Two was dealt with, there could be no closure.

We decided to leave the Strand One section of our document in the form of options on key issues, rather than a definitive text. That was the reality; it was not a final text, no matter what we said or how we described it.

The governments spent all of Monday in frantic negotiations on the annexes to Strand Two. Three years earlier, in the Frameworks Document, they had agreed on the need for new north-south institutions:

Both Governments consider that new institutions should be created to cater adequately for present and future political, social and economic inter-connections on the island of Ireland, enabling representatives of the main traditions, North and South, to enter agreed, dynamic, new, co-operative and constructive relationships.

Both Governments agree that these institutions should include a North/South body involving Heads of Department on both sides and duly established and maintained by legislation in both sovereign Parliaments. This body would bring together these Heads of Department representing the Irish Government and new democratic institutions in Northern Ireland, to discharge or oversee delegated executive, harmonizing or consultative functions as appropriate, over a range of matters which the two Governments designate in the first instance in agreement with the parties or which the two administrations, North and South, subsequently agree to designate. It is envi-

sioned that, in determining functions to be discharged or over-
seen by the North/South body, whether by executive action,
harmonization or consultation, account will be taken of:

>   (i) the common interest in a given matter on the part of
>   both parts of the island; or
>   (ii) the mutual advantage of addressing a matter together; or
>   (iii) the mutual benefit which may derive from it being ad-
>   ministered by the North/South body; or
>   (iv) the achievement of economies of scale and the avoid-
>   ance of unnecessary duplication of effort.[6]

London and Dublin were now trying to translate those objectives
into the reality of an agreement. The three annexes were to be lists
of subject areas in categories that corresponded to the words of
the Frameworks Document: executive, harmonizing, and consultative. It would, in any circumstance, have taken time to figure out
into which of those three categories to place agriculture, fisheries,
tourism, education, health policy, and dozens of other subject areas.
But the real problem was political. The British and Irish governments were the authors of the Frameworks Document. The nationalist parties supported it. The unionists did not—they had
loudly and repeatedly, in private and in public, made clear their
opposition.

Now, under intense time and political pressure, the Irish negotiators were trying to make the annexes as comprehensive as possible,
to hew as closely as they could to the Frameworks Document. The
British, on the other hand, recognized that the greater the fidelity to
the Frameworks Document the less likely it was that the Ulster
Unionists would accept the annexes and the agreement to which
they were to be attached. As a result, the negotiations lasted much
longer than anyone had anticipated. It was nearly midnight when we
got the annexes. I was surprised by their length and completeness.
They made the UUP's objection all the more certain.

Holkeri, de Chastelain, and I were once again in an awkward position. There had been tremendous pressure to get the document to
the parties by midnight so we could meet the Monday deadline. As
a result, we rushed when we should have paused. We should have
gone to bed and held the document overnight, to give us time to re-

view it and reflect on it. Instead, we hurried forward. I had the words "Draft Paper for Discussion" printed at the top of each page, and I wrote a covering memorandum explicitly describing it as just that, not as a document to be accepted or rejected. It would have been impossible to rewrite the Strand Two section at this late hour; in any event, we had already acceded to the governments' demand that we put it in without change.

It was after midnight when we met with the party leaders. It was a short session; they wanted to read the document. I made an emotional plea for them not to leak it. For the first and only time I used the word *beg;* I begged them not to use it for political advantage: the stakes were far too high for that. The future of the people of Northern Ireland for years, perhaps decades, would be decided by what they did in the next three days. It was an awesome responsibility, to which they could and must respond. Several of them echoed my remarks, pledging themselves and their parties to confidentiality. Fortunately, the document did not leak. The first document the press and public saw was the final agreement. By then what was in the earlier draft had no effect.

I knew the initial reaction would be negative. I hoped it could be quickly displaced by movement into serious, final negotiations. But I soon learned that I had underestimated how negative the reaction would be. The process now spun into a new crisis. John Taylor, the deputy leader of the UUP, told the press that he wouldn't touch the document with a forty-foot pole. Although it had been plainly and repeatedly described as a draft paper for discussion, the Ulster Unionists "rejected" the document. The PUP, the UDP, and the Alliance Party criticized it. Most of their wrath was directed at the Strand Two section, but they had other problems as well.

David Trimble released to the press a message he had delivered to Prime Minister Blair:

> This document is not something the UUP could recommend to the greater number of people in Northern Ireland for approval.
>
> Before contemplating alternative proposals, I wish to know from you and the Irish Government if you are prepared to consider radically different measures.[7]

It was painfully evident that there had been a breakdown in communication between Blair and Trimble. As Trimble later explained in an interview with the BBC:

> That night when we got the draft I quickly went through it, went to the Strand Two section, went to where the points that I'd been discussing with the Prime Minister, Monday morning, Saturday, looked for them. They weren't there. They weren't there. And what was there was a set of proposals that would bypass the Assembly. And what was there, at the end, were these huge, long lists. Annexes A, B and C, forty things I think in Annex A, sixteen in B, eight in C, for cross-border schemes and bodies, and what not, and all the rest of it. The pudding had been over egged, quite considerably. The minute we saw that we said, we've got a problem.[8]

Trimble then said that he immediately called Blair and

> . . . made it absolutely clear that there had to be a willingness to consider fundamental change, and in the absence of that willingness, then we would prefer not to get involved in negotiation and to say, well that's it.[9]

That was the crux of the matter. Before proceeding, Trimble wanted Blair and Ahern to commit themselves to renegotiate the Strand Two section, which they had negotiated just forty-eight hours earlier. Without that commitment, the talks were over.

On Tuesday morning, I met with Holkeri, de Chastelain, and our staff. We had all reached the same conclusion independently, so there was little discussion. We then went to the secretary of state's office for our daily meeting. I knew what had to be said. I didn't waste any time or mince any words. I reviewed what had happened on the Strand Two section. I then said, "It's the unanimous judgment of the independent chairmen that the prime ministers have to agree to renegotiate, in good faith, the Strand Two section. Otherwise these talks are over. We don't think Trimble is bluffing. He can't live with this." The British officials welcomed my statement.

They felt the same way. They had been uneasy with the prime ministers' negotiations from the outset.

It was much more difficult for the Irish. Their political strategy had been built on getting Sinn Fein into the talks and then negotiating an agreement which had the support of all of the nationalists at the table. Adherence to the Frameworks Document was a critical element in that strategy. Sinn Fein had said repeatedly that it would not support an accord that was seen as backsliding from the Frameworks Document. What the prime ministers had negotiated on Strand Two was based upon the Frameworks Document. If the Irish said no to renegotiation, the Ulster Unionists threatened to drop out and end the process. If they said yes to renegotiation it created the possibility of backing off from the Frameworks Document, and in that case Sinn Fein threatened to drop out. That meant, for the Irish government, the possibility, perhaps the probability, that a subsequent agreement would be rejected by nationalists, north and south. What I had just said had validated the unionist threat. It was my judgment that they were serious; they would walk out if there was no commitment to renegotiate.

David Andrews was the third foreign minister to lead the Irish government's delegation at the talks. Dick Spring had remained until a change of government in June 1997. Spring is handsome, intelligent, and effective. His very effectiveness made him unpopular with the unionists; they thought he was too "green." When Fianna Fail gained power at the head of a new coalition, Ahern appointed Ray Burke as foreign minister. Since Fianna Fail is, in the eyes of most unionists, the most green of all Irish parties, they were prepared to dislike Burke, but they quickly came to respect him. Blunt and charming, he was a man they could "do business" with. But Burke's tenure was cut short. He resigned from office over a matter unrelated to Northern Ireland and returned to private life.

Andrews succeeded Burke. An astute legislator and lawyer, he seemed a safe and reassuring choice. Unfortunately, he got off to a rocky start. In response to a reporter's question, he said that the new north-south bodies should have powers "not unlike a government." That set off alarm bells among the unionists, whose worst fear is precisely that those bodies will be the precursors of a united Ireland government. They criticized Andrews, and he was forced to backtrack. But gradually he regained his balance and confidence and, with Liz O'Donnell, who represented the Progressive Democratic Party, the junior party in the Irish government coalition, he had a steadying influence and made a valuable contribution to the process.

Andrews now handled this tense and difficult situation with tact and skill. There were no loud words, no threats, no recrimination. He thanked me for my comments, asked several questions, and then said he would communicate my views to his prime minister. I offered to call Ahern directly. Andrews said he didn't think that was necessary. A discussion ensued about whether and when the prime ministers should come to Stormont. The unanimous feeling was that they should appear as soon as possible.

The meeting broke up, and I returned to my office to see David Trimble. He had called early in the morning to request a one-on-one meeting. He was obviously upset. He began by dropping the document on the table in my office. Since it was more than sixty pages long, it made a loud, dramatic thud in the gloomy silence.

"It's a bad paper. A very bad paper."

"I know you feel that way, David. What's the biggest problem?"

"There are lots of problems. Strand Two. And the lists [annexes], the lists are too long, too detailed. The lists are simply unacceptable. The Irish government have got to agree to renegotiate this."

"I agree that they have to renegotiate."

"Will you tell them that?"

"I already have."

"They've got to agree to renegotiate, and it's got to be done fast."

It was a short meeting. It wasn't friendly, but Trimble wasn't rude or personally insulting. He was well aware that the Strand Two section to which he so strongly objected had been negotiated directly by the prime ministers. He told me then of his contact with Blair's office (he always referred to it as "Number 10") and the assurances he had received. I said the Strand Two section in the draft was word for word what had been given to me by the prime ministers, and that the annexes had been negotiated by the two governments' officials on Monday. He said he knew that. When he left, I felt confirmed in my earlier judgment. He wasn't bluffing—he couldn't accept this document as drafted. Blair would obviously be ready and willing, even anxious, to renegotiate the agreement. It was now up to Ahern.

Blair came to Northern Ireland that evening. Before leaving London he made a powerful statement, saying, among other things, "I feel the hand of history upon our shoulders." He spent the evening at the secretary of state's official residence at Hillsborough, a beautiful town just outside of Belfast. He had a round of meetings with many of the participants. We met with him late that night.

Blair possesses the elements of effective leadership in our era. He is intelligent, articulate, decisive, and photogenic. He knows the issues of Northern Ireland very well and has the courage to use his enormous political popularity to take risks for peace. His coming to Northern Ireland was a big gamble. There was no assurance of success, and most political consultants would have told him to stay away. But Blair came, and he had an immediate impact.

He had scheduled an early breakfast the next morning with Ahern. It was to be a critical meeting. Blair was ready to say that he was prepared to negotiate every part of the draft, including Strand Two. He was to ask Ahern to commit the Irish government to do the same. Blair had been briefed on our meeting earlier at Stormont. Although Andrews had felt that it was not necessary for me to call Ahern, Blair felt strongly that I should. "I think you should call Bertie," he said. "He should hear it directly from you." It was very late in the evening, and the breakfast was set for seven in the morning, but I promised to try to reach Ahern. As I left the meeting, I felt reassured by Blair's presence. He was making a total commitment, personal and political, to this negotiation. That didn't guarantee success, but without it there was no chance.

As soon as I got back to my hotel I tried but failed to reach Ahern. It was tremendously difficult for him. Not only was he directing the Irish government's participation in the negotiations, but his mother had died suddenly a few days earlier, so he was now planning her funeral as well. His schedule for the next day reflected his energy and his commitment. He left Dublin before sunrise to fly to Belfast for his breakfast meeting with Blair. He then came to Stormont for a series of meetings before returning to Dublin for his mother's funeral at noon. In the late afternoon he flew back to Belfast for another round of meetings that lasted into the early morning hours of the next day. I was with him at two o'clock that next morning. I don't recall ever having seen a person as totally exhausted. I also had never seen a person more determined. As we sat in his office talking, his face was gray with exhaustion. But his eyes burned like hot coals as he said to me: "George, we've got to get this done. We've got to get this done."

That we were in a position to get it done was due to Ahern's courage and dedication. Just twenty-four hours earlier the process had teetered at the edge of collapse. On Tuesday evening, Ahern had been in Dublin getting ready to attend a last church service in honor of his mother when he was interrupted by a group of his aides. They were uncomfortable bothering him at such a sad and personal time, but there was a crisis at Stormont and they needed direction from the top. They briefed him on the events of that day: the eruption of unionist opposition to the draft agreement and their demand to renegotiate the Strand Two section he had agreed on with Blair just two days earlier. Ahern's aides recommended that he reject the demand. They felt that Dublin had negotiated in good faith with London, and an agreement had been reached by the prime ministers. They urged that the efforts of the two governments be devoted to persuading the political parties to accept that agreement, not toward renegotiating it. Ahern agreed. "Tell them to stand firm," he said, and he left for the church.

After the service he went for a long walk. Trailed at a discreet distance by his security detail, alone with his thoughts, he strolled the streets of his native Dublin. He knew every street, every storefront. His thoughts alternated between his beloved mother, whom he would bury tomorrow, and the negotiations at Stormont, which he desperately wanted to keep alive. Just two hours earlier he had decided not to renegotiate and not to go to Stormont the next morning. Now, he reconsidered that decision. With his mother's funeral scheduled for noon it would be extremely inconvenient for him to go to Stormont to meet Blair at seven in the morning and then to return to Dublin for the service. But he would do it. He had to do it. Too many lives were at stake. The negotiations could not be allowed to fail.

Ahern took his portable telephone out of his pocket and called his top aide, Paddy Teahon. He told Teahon that he had decided to go to Stormont to meet Blair for breakfast and asked him to make the necessary arrangements. At ten o'clock at night, standing alone on a dark and silent Dublin street, the prime minister of the Republic of Ireland made the decision: the Irish government would agree to renegotiate on Strand Two. It was a big decision by a big man. It made possible everything that followed.

Had Ahern insisted on the Strand Two provisions he had worked out with Blair, there would not have been a Good Friday Agreement. Ahern could have said to Blair: "We made a deal and I insist on sticking to it. I sold it to the nationalists. You must sell it to the unionists." But he didn't. He recognized the reality that the unionists would not accept it. So Ahern agreed to renegotiate.

It was a momentous risk. Had the talks collapsed because of a British-unionist disagreement over Strand Two, they would have been blamed for the failure and for the bitter conflict that everyone assumed would follow. By agreeing to renegotiate, Ahern averted that, but he created the possibility of a fatal split among nationalists. The SDLP and Sinn Fein approved of the Blair-Ahern deal on Strand Two. To renegotiate it to accommodate unionist objections inevitably meant, for the nationalists, giving something up. It is an understatement to say that in the politics of Northern Ireland there is not a tradition of anybody giving anything up. If the process failed now, it could be the nationalists, particularly Ahern, who got the blame.

Ahern and Blair now set out to make enough modifications to Strand Two to get the unionists on board, without losing the nationalists. They were helped by the fact that Sinn Fein was deeply concerned about the release of prisoners. Over the previous twenty-five years of conflict, hundreds of members of paramilitary organizations—republican and loyalist—had been convicted of violent crimes and imprisoned. Now, as part of any agreement, republicans and loyalists wanted their prisoners to be released. So in dealing with them, Ahern and Blair had to focus on the section of the agreement regarding prisoners while they were dealing with the Ulster Unionists on Strand Two.

It was a high-wire act. A misstep would have ended the negotiations. But Blair and Ahern never faltered. Calmly and steadily, step by careful step, they got across the divide safely. It was a superb demonstration of leadership.

From the time of their breakfast, at seven on Wednesday morning, until nearly five on Friday afternoon, a total of fifty-eight hours, there were few pauses in the discussions. Blair took over a suite of offices on the top floor of the government office building in which the talks were held, just a few steps down the hall from my office. On the floor below, Ahern set up in the Irish government's offices. Up and down and back and forth the parties went, ricocheting from meeting to meeting, clutching documents, wielding pens, wagging fingers at each other. Strand Two got much of the attention. But there was a lot of haggling on almost every section of the document. Decommissioning, as ever, was controversial. The unionists, deeply frustrated by the failure to as yet achieve any handover of arms, pressed for an early deadline and tougher requirements. They wanted a provision that would prevent Sinn Fein from participating in the new Assembly executive (the equivalent of a cabinet) unless the IRA handed over some arms. It wouldn't have affected the loyalists, since no one expected them to win enough seats in the new Assembly to be eligible to participate in the executive; Sinn Fein almost certainly would, however. The unionists didn't receive everything they wanted in the agreement, but they eventually got a letter from Blair dealing with the concerns they had raised.

Even more emotional than decommissioning was the subject of prisoners. For Sinn Fein and the loyalist parties this was a concern of surpassing importance. David Ervine and his PUP colleagues, and Gary McMichael and the UDP delegates all fought hard and insistently for a prompt release program. Gerry Adams and Martin McGuinness were dogged on the issue. I had to smile at one late-night scene in the hallway, just outside my office: Bertie Ahern, trying to make his way downstairs after a meeting with Blair; Gerry Adams holding on to Ahern's sleeve, pulling him back up the stairs, trying to get in another few words on prisoners. In the end, the language on prisoners was acceptable to Sinn Fein and the loyalists, but it was deeply offensive to many unionists. They were adamantly opposed to the early release of prisoners; they wanted them to serve their full terms in prison.

As we worked to bring the talks to a successful conclusion, men of violence worked to destroy them. In Londonderry, thirty-four-year-old Trevor Deeney was shot to death. According to press reports, he was believed to be a member of the LVF. The INLA claimed responsibility.[10] But the murder had no effect on the talks; too much momentum had been generated. The finish line was in sight.

I met with Blair on Tuesday night and with Ahern on Wednesday. I told them that the one thing I wanted from them was an absolute commitment to the deadline. I said:

When we start on Thursday morning, it has to be clear to everyone that we'll continue until we finish, one way or the other. There can be no discussion of a pause or a break. I intend to tell the parties that I won't even consider such a request. If someone says to me, "We're nearly there but we're all tired, let's break until next week," I'm going to say "That's completely out of the question. There's not going to be a break, not for a week, not for a day, not for an hour. We're here until we finish. We'll either get an agreement or we'll fail to get an agreement. Then we'll all go out together and explain to the press and the waiting world how we succeeded or why we failed."

Blair and Ahern agreed, without hesitation. They knew the importance of the deadline. I delivered the message to all of the delegates. My hopes surged.

Trimble was in a very difficult situation. Ahern had opened the door to the last phase of the talks by his decision to renegotiate on Strand Two. But Trimble carried not only the immediate burden of renegotiation—how many north-south bodies? how were they to be created? what would be the scope of their authority?—he was also being attacked daily by Paisley and McCartney, and some members of his own party, all of whom accused him of selling out the union. And he was carrying the burden of history, as seen through unionist eyes. For them it had been a long, painful slide from a position of dominance to one of being besieged, accompanied by (to many, caused by) a maddening campaign of murder by violent republicans. Although they called themselves British, and wanted only to be British, they watched with growing anger as the British govern-

ment, *their* government, made what they saw as unprincipled concessions to terrorism. Many years earlier Trimble himself had
helped bring down the last unionist government which had given up
too much to nationalism.

In 1973 and 1974, talks involving the British and Irish governments and the constitutional parties of Northern Ireland concluded
in what became known as the Sunningdale Agreement (after the location in England in which the negotiations took place). Under that
pact, the Ulster Unionists agreed to share power with the SDLP
and the Alliance Party. There was also to be created a Council of
Ireland, which unionists feared would exercise executive functions.
Paisley led a coalition of unionists in opposition, a protest strike
crippled Northern Ireland, and in an election held in 1974 unionists
who supported the agreement were routed. The prime minister,
Brian Faulkner, was forced to resign, his political career over. A
young Catholic named John Hume had served in Faulkner's short-
lived cabinet. And a young Protestant named David Trimble had
been active in opposition to Faulkner and the agreement.

Now in an ironic turn of the wheel of history, Trimble was trying
to negotiate the accommodation necessary to end decades of war in
a climate of fear and hostility, amid constant cries of betrayal. What
he had going for him, of course, was the desperate longing for peace
and normality that existed across Northern Ireland, among both
unionists and nationalists. Twenty-five years of brutal sectarian war
had scarred the bodies of thousands of men and women; it had more
deeply scarred the hearts of everyone. It wasn't so much the numbers killed (3,200) and wounded (36,000). It was the fear, the anxiety, which gnawed away at every soul. The highly publicized and
emotional funeral had become a regular event in Northern Ireland.
The vast majority of people had had enough of that. They were sick
of it. They wanted change.

Trimble also benefitted from the willingness of many unionists to
accept change. They knew that there could never be a return to the
dominant days of the past. Of course, not all unionists feel this way.
Some do yearn for the past. Some steadfastly deny any previous discrimination. To them, all of the problems were caused by republican
terrorists and agitators who created a false history to advance their

goal of a united Ireland. The rhetoric of this faction of unionism had always been enough to stoke nationalist fears and unionist grievances.

Through the day on Thursday, April 9, and on into the night, the parties moved closer to agreement. Blair and Ahern played a central role in these negotiations. They obviously had developed a warm personal relationship; that made progress possible. They didn't just supervise the negotiations; they conducted them. Word by word, sentence by sentence, paragraph by paragraph, the compromise came together.

The key section of the final agreement on Strand Two was, in the very best sense of the words, a principled compromise. The long lists contained in the three annexes were sharply reduced to a single annex with twelve subject areas. In retrospect, it is clear that the earlier Blair-Ahern discussions had in a very short time forced the issue on Strand Two. Controversial as they were, without those negotiations it is likely that we would not have been able to finish Strand Two by the deadline. On the crucial issue of authority, a delicate balance was struck. The British and Irish governments made an absolute commitment to establish a North/South Ministerial Council and to create "implementation bodies" to carry out the council's decisions. The difficult issue of timing and authority was resolved by the creation of a "transitional" phase, during which the ministerial council, the new Northern Ireland Assembly, and a new British/Irish Council would simultaneously and cooperatively begin to function. Any expansion of these arrangements would have to be approved by the Assembly.

The compromise was sealed by the inclusion of what Blair labeled "a mutual destruction" provision. The unionists wanted an Assembly; the nationalists wanted north-south institutions. The unionists feared that the nationalists would work to make the north-south institutions function and then sabotage the Assembly; that was why the unionists insisted that the north-south institutions be subordinate to the Assembly. The nationalists had the opposite concern: that the unionists would work to make the Assembly function and then undermine the north-south institutions; that was why the nationalists wanted those institutions created directly by the British and Irish Parliaments, independent of the Assembly. To ease the concerns of both sides, the agreement makes the institutions "mutually inter-dependent" and stipulates "that one cannot successfully function without the other."[11] To emphasize the point, a sentence to the same effect was added to the introductory "Declaration of Support."[12]

Although Ahern had gambled when he agreed to renegotiate his agreement with Blair on Strand Two, in the end he and everyone else came out much further ahead, for an agreement was now possible. Even within the narrow confines of Strand Two, the final product was a vast improvement for everyone, including nationalists. It had the benefit of direct input from all of the participants. They modified it and made it more realistic and acceptable—and therefore more likely to endure.

Once Strand Two was settled I felt that we were nearing the finish line. As we had anticipated, the Ulster Unionists were ready to talk on Strand One as soon as they were satisfied on Strand Two. Under Paul Murphy's leadership, they and the SDLP settled in for a long night of haggling over the details of the new Assembly. Mark Durban and Sean Farren of the SDLP played key roles in this phase of the negotiations. As I had also anticipated, the unionists were ready to accept power-sharing. Under the agreement, key decisions will require the support of the elected representatives of both communities; there will have to be:

> (i) *either* parallel consent *i.e.* a majority of those members present and voting including a majority of the unionist and nationalist designations present and voting;
> (ii) *or* a weighted majority (60%) of members present and voting including at least 40% of each of the nationalist and unionist designations present and voting.[13]

Late Thursday night, a sad spectacle unfolded on the fringe of the negotiations. In a last-ditch effort to block an agreement, Ian Paisley led a few hundred of his supporters onto the grounds at Stormont. Angry at being denied entrance, they broke through a gate and surged up the hill to a monument to the legendary unionist leader Edward Carson. According to press reports, some were

masked, and many carried British flags. They called Trimble a traitor and denounced the talks.[14] Following a discussion with British
officials, it was agreed that the crowd would disperse if Paisley could
hold a press conference. Several of us interrupted our discussions to
watch the press conference, which was carried live on television.
Paisley and some of his colleagues from the DUP sat at a table;
others stood behind him. As he tried to make a statement he was interrupted by loud, rude heckling. Some members of the loyalist parties, once among the most fervent of his supporters, savagely
accused him of running away. They told him that earlier in their
lives they had listened to him, but no more. He was the ghost of a
violent past, now they wanted peace. Go home, they chanted, go
home. It was a demeaning performance. Watching with us were several government officials with long experience in Northern Ireland.
One of them said softly, "Once he would have brought thousands,
tens of thousands with him. Now he has a few hundred. And look at
those loyalists. Many of them thought him a god. They went out
and killed, thinking they were saving the union. Now they've turned
on him. It's the end of an era." Paisley left the press conference. The
negotiations ground on.

Midnight came and went. We had missed the deadline, but we
were driving to a conclusion. I went to Blair's office, then down one
flight of stairs to where Ahern was working. I then went back upstairs
to Mowlam's office, and walked back to my office. Paul Murphy gave
me a briefing on the Strand One talks between the UUP and the
SDLP. "They're haggling but they're going to get it done," he told
me. As I went from meeting to meeting, I gained a sense of growing
hope, of accelerating optimism. At about five in the morning, I
walked down the hall to take a shower. With Blair's visit had come
the revelation that just outside the office he was using was a small
room with a shower. I had been working in this building for nearly
two years and I hadn't known of the existence of this room, barely
twenty-five steps from my office. I hadn't washed, showered, or
changed for twenty-four hours. I was dragging so much I wasn't de-
terred by the mess in the tiny room. It looked as though everyone in
the building had used it that night. The floor was covered with water.
A pile of used towels was stacked along one wall. The mirror was
completely fogged by steam. There was no dry place to put my

clothes when I took them off. But none of that mattered. As I stood under the showerhead, letting the hot water roll over me, I had one thought: We're going to do it! We're going to do it! For two long years, two difficult years, two seemingly endless years, we had kept at it, even when most people thought it was hopeless. Now, it was about to end, and we were going to get an agreement. My eyes misted over, and my tears mingled with the water running down my face.

At 8:15 on Friday morning (3:15 a.m. in Washington), I received a telephone call from President Clinton.

"What're you doing up so late?" I asked.

"I can't sleep. I want to know what's happening. I want to help."

We talked for about a half hour. I reviewed the status of the talks and described the sticking points. Clinton had talked to Blair and Ahern and had a good grasp of the problems. We discussed each of the key participants and what he might say to them. It didn't take much briefing on my part. He knew each of the negotiators so well that he called them all by their first names, and he was already well aware of the issues. He then phoned Trimble, Hume, Adams, and others. The calls were very helpful. The delegates knew the president well from their prior meetings with him. They knew how well he understood the issues. They were impressed that he would stay up all night, to follow the negotiations, to talk with them.

My tiredness gave way to a burst of energy and enthusiasm. Now, as I encountered delegates in meetings, in the hallway, in the bathroom, they asked, quietly, hesitantly, almost fearfully: Is it possible, after all? Are we that close? Can we really do it? It was emotional. It was moving.

And it was premature.

There was one last obstacle to overcome. When Trimble received the final draft on Friday morning, he took it apart and distributed sections of it to the ten or twelve members of his negotiating team. So many other party leaders and members had come to Stormont that the room assigned to the UUP was now overcrowded. So they took over adjacent space which had been used by the UKUP; it had been vacant since McCartney and his colleagues had walked out months earlier. There was real irony in that: the UUP making a decision critical to its future, and that of Northern Ireland, in the office of its bitter rival.

After they had gone through the document, section by section, line by line, they listed and discussed their objections. There were many, but two were critical: the release of prisoners; and whether or not Sinn Fein would be able to serve in the executive of the new Assembly if, by the time of its formation, the IRA had not yet decommissioned any weapons. The UUP needed reassurance on those two issues. So they went to the only place they felt they could get that reassurance.

At about mid-afternoon, five of the highest UUP officials, led by Trimble, met with Blair. They laid out their concerns. With consummate skill and understanding, Blair reassured them. He could not at this late stage change the agreement, especially the section on prisoners. But he would put his reassuring words into a side letter.

The Ulster Unionists returned to their office, where they briefed their party colleagues. There had been many interruptions to their meeting, and they knew time was running out, so they locked the door. Blair quickly prepared and signed the letter of reassurance and dispatched a top aide to deliver it to Trimble. But when the aide arrived at the UUP office, the door was locked and he could not get in. Unaware that the letter itself was outside trying to get in, Trimble and his colleagues continued to discuss it behind the locked door. Finally, the aide got the attention of someone near the door. The letter was handed to Trimble, who read it and handed it to John Taylor. He read it and passed it around to the party leaders.

The letter from Blair to Trimble read:

I understand your problem with paragraph 25 of Strand 1 is that it requires decisions on those who should be excluded or removed from office in the Northern Ireland Executive to be taken on a cross-community basis.

This letter is to let you know that if, during the course of the first six months of the shadow Assembly or the Assembly itself, these provisions have been shown to be ineffective, we will support changes to these provisions to enable them to be made properly effective in preventing such people from holding office.

Furthermore, I confirm that in our view the effect of the decommissioning section of the agreement, with decommissioning schemes coming into effect in June, is that the process of decommissioning should begin straight away.

Most of the leaders seemed satisfied. After more intense debate among the talks team and the others in the room, Trimble ended the discussion. "It's my intention to call George Mitchell and tell him that we're ready to proceed." And he did.

Why did Trimble take that fateful step? He, like every other human being, is a complex mixture of hopes and fears, dreams and anxieties, biases and prejudices. He, like every political leader I have ever met, mixes high ideals, wanting "to do good," with driving ambition, wanting "to be recognized." He ended up accomplishing both. Each day of the nearly two years of the negotiations was for him a struggle to avoid being thrown off balance. Attacked daily by some unionists for selling out the union, criticized often by some nationalists for recalcitrance, he threaded his way through a minefield of problems, guided by his intelligence, his sure grasp of the political situation, and his determination to reach agreement. I believe that, in the end, Trimble did the right thing for the right reason: he saw the opportunity to end a long and bitter conflict, and he did not want to go down in the history books as the man who let it pass.

Trimble was able to override the dissension in the UUP because he had the support of his party's most senior and influential members. John Taylor, the deputy leader, is a member of Parliament; known for his gruff demeanor and tough talk, he is a shrewd and skillful negotiator. Ken Maginnis is also a member of Parliament and the party's security spokesman; a former officer in the Ulster Defence Regiment, he is regarded as a moderate on cross-community issues. Reg Empey, a former lord mayor of Belfast, was able to reach across the divide that separates the two communities; as a result, he was respected by all of the participants in the negotiations.

Trimble called me at 4:45 p.m. and told me that the Ulster Unionists "were ready to do the business." I asked my staff to immediately notify the governments and the other parties that we would meet in plenary session at five o'clock to vote on the agreement. We had met in this room many times before. But this time it was different. The shape of the table was changed from square to rectangular, to take up less room. That made it possible to let in some of the hundreds of the members of the parties who had come to witness history in the making. The place was packed with people standing, in a solid mass, behind the seated delegates.

For the first time there were television cameras in the room. The British government's Northern Ireland Office had worked out a media plan to permit an announcement to be made immediately after the vote. But the technicians jumped the gun, and the proceedings went live several minutes before the vote. So as the world watched, the governments and the parties voted for the agreement. Sinn Fein had to wait a few weeks for an endorsement by its party convention, but Gerry Adams's words were encouraging and supportive. It was one of the most emotional moments of my life, but I tried to remain calm as I made the announcement.

I'm pleased to announce that the two Governments, and the political parties of Northern Ireland, have reached agreement. The agreement proposes changes in the Irish Constitution and in British constitutional law to enshrine the principle that it is the people of Northern Ireland who will decide, democratically, their own future. The agreement creates new institutions: a Northern Ireland Assembly, to restore to the people the fundamental democratic right to govern themselves; and a North/South Council, to encourage cooperation and joint action for mutual benefit. It deals fairly with such sensitive issues as prisoners, policing, and decommissioning.

This agreement is good for the people of Ireland, North and South. It was made possible by the leadership, commitment, and, in these last few days, the personal negotiating skill of Prime Minister Tony Blair and the Taoiseach, Bertie Ahern. Their commitment has been evident by their presence here for days, their hands-on style, their all-night effort, and we're honored by their presence.

If the agreement is approved in referendums North and South, it offers the chance for a better future. But to secure that future it will take the good-faith efforts of the leaders gathered here, and the commitment of all the people of Northern Ireland. Making the Assembly work, making the North/South Council effective, will test these leaders as much as did getting this agreement. The people of Northern Ireland will make the difference.

This agreement proves that democracy works, and in its wake we can say to the men of violence, to those who disdain democracy, whose tools are bombs and bullets: Your way is not the right way. You will never solve the problems of Northern Ireland by violence. You will only make them worse.

It doesn't take courage to shoot a policeman in the back of the head, or to murder an unarmed taxi driver. What takes courage is to compete in the arena of democracy, where the tools are persuasion, fairness, and common decency. You should help to build this society instead of tearing it apart. You can learn something from some of the lives you've destroyed, like those of Damian Trainor and Philip Allen. They were two young men, best friends, who saw each other as human beings, not as a Protestant and a Catholic. Philip was to be married with Damian as his best man. Instead they lie buried, near each other, sharing death as they shared life, victims last month of a brutal and senseless murder. Their deaths showed what Northern Ireland has had to endure. Their lives showed what Northern Ireland can be.

This agreement points the way. For that, credit must go to many people, especially those here today. We will shortly hear from each of the political leaders of Northern Ireland. Let me first speak of them collectively. They have negotiated tirelessly for two years. They've constantly had to strike a balance between their obligations to their constituents and the needs of the larger society. That's hard to do in any democracy; it's especially difficult in this divided society.

Through it all they kept their sense of purpose. And they delivered an agreement that's fair and balanced and offers hope to the people of Northern Ireland. For that they deserve the gratitude of their people and the just verdict of history.

I was very tired, but I could not have been happier. We had gotten an agreement, and I would be home in time to spend Easter

Sunday with my family, to take Heather and Andrew for a walk in Central Park.

The stories in Saturday's newspapers were mostly positive. "Ulster chooses hope over hate" (the *Times* of London). "Peace at last for Ulster" (the *Independent*). "The new beginning, Historic day as peace deal is sealed at last" (*Irish Independent*). For the first time in a long time it was a pleasure to read the papers over breakfast.

I had interviews with several reporters that morning in the lobby of the hotel. The last one was with David Lynch of *USA Today*. After we finished, I said good-bye to and thanked the hotel staff. David and I then walked out of the hotel and across the parking lot toward the car that waited to take me to the airport. I said good-bye to David and opened the car door. Suddenly, someone called my name. I turned to see two elderly, gray-haired women walking toward me. One of them grabbed my hands and said, "We want to thank you. Not for us, our lives are nearly over, but for our grandchildren, whose lives are just beginning. Thanks to you they'll lead lives of peace and hope, something we've never known." Then, with tears of joy streaming down their faces, they hugged me.

Those words will echo in my mind forever. They made it all worthwhile.

CHAPTER 16

Peace

MY most fervent prayer is that history will record that the
Troubles ended in Omagh on the sunny afternoon of Saturday, August 15, 1998. There, a murderous explosion laid bare for all
to see the brutality, the senselessness, the utter insanity of political
violence in Northern Ireland. The graves of the twenty-nine men,
women, and children who lost their lives on that fateful day should
mark the closure of a violent era in the deeply troubled history
of Northern Ireland. The emblems of the passing of that era will be
a thirty-three-year-old man and a fifteen-year-old girl. The man,
Michael Monaghan, lost his eighteen-month-old daughter, his
pregnant wife, and his wife's mother to that mad spasm of political
violence. He now struggles to raise his three remaining children,
including two-year-old Patrick, who asks his father every day,
"When's Mommy coming home?" The fifteen-year-old girl is
Claire Gallagher, who lost her eyes in the blast. Now she sits, tall
and lovely, her eyes covered by huge white bandages, no longer able
to play the piano, trying to be brave. Michael and Claire are brave in
the way their assailants never could be—decent, honorable, ordinary citizens, whose lives have been forever damaged; yet they ask
for peace, for reconciliation.

Within days of the Omagh atrocity, the few dissident groups which
had, until then, opposed the Good Friday Agreement, announced the
cessation of violence. For the first time in thirty years, all of the paramilitary organizations operating in Northern Ireland declared a
cease-fire or suspended military operations. As I write these words,
late in 1998, an uncertain peace has fallen across Northern Ireland. It

is a fragile peace, which could end at any time; there are many crucial decisions yet to be made.

I am not objective. I am deeply biased in favor of the people of Northern Ireland. Having spent three and a half years among them, I've come to like and admire them, to enjoy being with them. Among other things, they are large of heart and they learn from their mistakes. David Ervine learned from his mistakes. Born in 1953 in Belfast to working-class parents, Ervine was motivated to take up loyalist violence by an act of republican violence. When he was nineteen, the IRA exploded a series of bombs across Belfast on what has become known as Bloody Friday. Nine people died. One of them was a man also named David Ervine who lived across the street, although he was no relation. Ervine decided to join the paramilitaries. "I felt that my society was under siege, being attacked. I had a young son then, and I wanted to end the pain. I felt to do that, I would have to participate in the war." He became a member of the Ulster Volunteer Force (UVF) and joined their campaign of violence. Two years later, while driving a stolen car packed with a bomb, he was stopped and arrested. "The army officer tied a rope around my ankle and demanded that I took the bomb out of the car, he was afraid of being booby-trapped. In court he gave me credit, dubious credit I suppose, for defusing the bomb. I don't think the judge was impressed by it."

He spent the next six years in prison, where he met Gusty Spence. The former leader of the UVF, Spence had been one of the most violent and articulate of loyalists, best known for his chilling instruction: "If you can't get an IRA man, get a Taig [Catholic], he's your last resort." Once in prison, Spence underwent a transformation, and he used his immense power of persuasion to convert men of violence into missionaries for peace. Ervine became one of those missionaries. After his release from prison he joined the Progressive Unionist Party. Stocky and balding, with a bushy mustache, his energy and skill propelled him to political leadership. He gained entry to the negotiations in the election of May 1996 and was elected to the Northern Ireland Assembly in June 1998. While passionately devoted to the union, he has no hesitancy about talking with Sinn Fein, or anyone else, in the search for a society of peace and equality.

His earthy candor serves as a magnet for reporters looking for a colorful story. He once described Seamus Mallon as "skillful, incisive and brutal. He could take somebody's scrotum, slice off their balls, it would be over in a second and they wouldn't know it was done, such is his skill." Ervine engaged in one of the more dramatic exchanges in the negotiations. Before Paisley and McCartney left the talks in July 1997, they often denounced the entire process. They particularly resented it being called a peace process, because they felt it had not and would not bring peace to Northern Ireland. McCartney argued that to the contrary, the process contributed to violence, and he demanded that it be ended. On one occasion, while making this point during an especially heated debate, McCartney said with emotion: "If this be peace let us have war." Ervine cut in immediately, with equal passion: "That's easy for you to say, safe as you and your family are in the suburbs. But if there's war it's we and our sons who'll do the fighting and dying. We want this process because it's our only hope for peace."

That statement captured Ervine's advocacy for the Protestant working class, which he felt had been exploited during the conflict. "If only 3 percent of Protestant working-class kids passed the eleven-plus [exams], what sort of ascendancy is that?" he once asked.

Ervine and others made an important contribution to the peace process. As a result of my experience with them, I have come to believe more deeply than ever before in the power of human redemption. I saw and worked with men who in their youth committed brutal acts of violence, including murder, with the faith that they were fighting for their families and for their community's way of life. Convicted and punished, they spent long years in prison where they came under the influence of men like Gusty Spence. They left prison committed to peace and equality. They do not deny their violent pasts. They acknowledge them frankly, but they argue convincingly that they paid for and learned from their mistakes; now they want to atone for them.

The entire society learned from its mistakes. They learned that violence won't solve their problems, it will only make them worse. They learned that unionists and nationalists have more things in common than they have differences. They learned that knowledge of their history is a good thing but being chained to the past is not. Finally, they came to believe—with good reason—that peace and political stability will enable them to enjoy unprecedented growth and prosperity.

I think that the Good Friday Agreement will endure. There will be many setbacks along the way, but the direction for Northern Ireland is firmly set. No society in human history has been able to enjoy the complete absence of violence. Our own American society, of which we are justly proud, is regularly scarred by horrific acts of violence. So it is unfair and unrealistic to hold the people of Northern Ireland to a standard that has never been met elsewhere. There will be among them the deranged, the regressive, the criminal. Individuals will die in early and untimely ways. But the organized political violence of the past thirty years, which killed and injured thousands, is over for now.

Whether it is over for good depends on the people of Northern Ireland and the quality of their leaders. I have faith in both. The political leaders rose to the occasion on Good Friday, in the most difficult of circumstances. I have seen, close up, what they are made of and what they are capable of doing. I'm hopeful that, despite the inevitable human errors, they will conduct the affairs of Northern Ireland in a way that will build trust and confidence among the people.

If the Good Friday Agreement endures, it will be because it is fair and balanced. It is based on the principle that the future of Northern Ireland should be decided by the people of Northern Ireland, and it seeks to promote tolerance and mutual respect. It includes constitutional change in the Republic of Ireland and in the United Kingdom. It creates new democratic institutions to provide self-governance in the north and to encourage cooperation between the north and south for their mutual benefit. It explicitly repudiates the use or threat of violence for any political purpose and commits its signatories and supporters to the total disarmament of all paramilitary organizations.

It is a long document, and it covers many complex issues. But the principles which underlie it are few in number and simple in concept; those principles are also universal in their reach and importance. For that reason, when the people voted on May 22, 1998, they knew what they were voting on. They might have disagreed with a detail here and a provision there, but they understood that they were voting for peace, for tolerance, for mutual respect. Most of all, they were voting for their children, for a future not filled with fear and anxiety, not marked by random, senseless death.

In the first all-island vote in eighty years, 85 percent of those who voted said yes (95 percent in the Republic of Ireland, 71 percent in Northern Ireland). It was, by any measure, an impressive affirmation of the agreement. More than anything else, it is that overwhelming public support, freely given in an open, democratic election, that instills in me the hope that the Troubles are over.

The people of Ireland are sick of war. They are sick of sectarian killings and random bombings. They are sick of the sad elegance of funerals, especially those involving the small white coffins of children, prematurely laid into the rolling green fields of the Irish countryside. They want peace.

The Good Friday Agreement was, for me, the realization of a dream that sustained me for three and a half years, the longest, most difficult years of my life. After the agreement was approved, I talked with several of the men and women who had negotiated it; we were all overcome with exhaustion and emotion. As we parted, I told them that I have a new dream.

That dream is to return to Northern Ireland in a few years with my young son, Andrew. We will roam the countryside, taking in the sights and smells and sounds of one of the most beautiful landscapes on earth. Then, on a rainy afternoon (there are many in Northern Ireland) we will drive to Stormont and sit quietly in the visitors gallery of the Northern Ireland Assembly. There we will watch and listen as the members of the Assembly debate the ordinary issues of life in a peaceful democratic society: education, health care, agriculture, tourism, fisheries, trade. There will be no talk of war, for the war will have long been over. There will be no talk of peace, for peace will by then be taken for granted. On that day, the day on which peace is taken for granted in Northern Ireland, I will be fulfilled.

Notes

CHAPTER 2

1. Terminology in Northern Ireland is a minefield. There is no universally accepted word or phrase to describe those nationalists who support or condone the use of force to expel the British from Northern Ireland. The words "the republican movement" are most often used for that purpose, although some members of that movement deny that they support or condone the use of force, and some nationalists who are not part of the republican movement may at different times tolerate or support the use of force.

2. The treaty was signed in December 1921 and took effect in 1922.

3. Taoiseach (pronounced tee-shuck) is the Irish word for leader. The literal translation is "chief."

4. The four parties were the Alliance, the SDLP, the Ulster Unionist Party, and the Democratic Unionist Party.

CHAPTER 4

1. *Irish Times,* January 25, 1996.

CHAPTER 5

1. *Irish News,* June 10, 1996.

2. *Irish News,* June 11, 1996.

3. Dennis Cooke, *Persecuting Zeal* (Dingle, County Kerry: Brandon, 1996), p. 36.

4. Ibid., p. 219. "Two themes have been central to Ian Paisley's teaching and preaching on the Roman Catholic Church: firstly, and very simply, the Roman Catholic Church is not a Christian Church; and secondly, Roman Catholicism is an instigator of persecution and revolution throughout the world and has been behind the 'Troubles' in Northern Ireland" (Ibid., p. 41).

5. Ibid., p. 63.

6. Ibid., p. 69.

7. Ibid., p. 164.

8. Ibid., p. 1.

9. Ibid., p. 202.

10. *News Letter,* November 30, 1998.

11. Cooke, p. 204.

12. *The Irish News,* November 30, 1998.
13. *Irish Independent,* June 13, 1996.
14. *Belfast Telegraph,* July 8, 1996.
15. Ibid.
16. *News Letter,* July 9, 1996.
17. *Irish News,* July 12, 1996. The *News Letter* is generally considered to be conservative unionist, the *Belfast Telegraph* moderate unionist.
18. *Guardian,* July 12, 1996.
19. *News Letter,* July 29, 1996.

CHAPTER 6

1. The participants constantly referred to such allegations as indictments. But they were not in any sense legal documents. They were usually brief typewritten statements, drawn from and supported by newspaper articles.

CHAPTER 7

1. *Belfast Telegraph,* October 8, 1996.

CHAPTER 9

1. *News Letter,* December 2, 1996.
2. *Sunday World,* December 1, 1996.
3. *Sunday Express,* December 1, 1996.
4. *Mail on Sunday* and *Sunday World,* December 1, 1996.
5. *Belfast Telegraph,* December 2, 1996.
6. *News Letter,* December 2, 1996.
7. *Irish News,* December 2, 1996.
8. *New York Post,* December 2, 1996.
9. *Irish News,* December 3, 1996.
10. Ibid.
11. *Sunday World,* December 8, 1996.
12. *Sunday Tribune,* December 8, 1996.

CHAPTER 10

1. *Belfast Telegraph,* February 13, 1997.

CHAPTER 11

1. *News Letter,* May 17, 1997.
2. *News Letter,* May 17, 1997.
3. The results of several recent elections are fairly consistent. On the unionist side, the Ulster Unionist Party is the largest (it is also the largest party in Northern Ireland), followed closely by the Democratic Unionist Party; then there is a sharp drop to the much smaller United Kingdom Unionist Party and the two loyalist parties, the Progressive Unionist Party and the Ulster Democratic Party. On the nationalist side, the Social Democratic and Labour Party is the largest (it is the second largest party in Northern Ireland), followed by Sinn Fein. In total, these parties regularly gained over 90 percent of the votes. The remaining votes are divided

among parties which are nonaligned, the largest of which is the Alliance Party. Although the Northern Ireland Women's Coalition has been in existence only since 1996, it has made an impressive start; it obtained enough votes in the 1996 election to gain entry into the negotiations, and then, in the election of June 1998, won two seats in the new Assembly. Also created in 1996 was the Labour Party (unrelated to the British Labour Party), which did well enough to get into the negotiations but was unable to win any seats in the Assembly.

CHAPTER 12

1. *Independent*, July 22, 1997.
2. *The Times*, July 22, 1997.
3. *Belfast Telegraph*, July 22, 1997.
4. *Irish Times*, July 24, 1997.
5. Gerry Adams, *Before the Dawn* (London: Mandarin, 1997), p. 51.
6. John de Chastelain was appointed chairman. The other members are Ambassador Donald Johnson, an American career foreign service officer, and Brigadier Tauno Nieminen, a retired Finnish military officer.
7. Statement in the Dail (the Irish Parliament) on September 11, 1997.
8. *Irish News*, September 11, 1997.

CHAPTER 13

1. *News Letter*, December 17, 1997.

CHAPTER 14

1. *The Times*, December n.d., 1997.
2. *News Letter*, January 2, 1998.
3. *News Letter*, January 7, 1998.
4. *News Letter*, January 10, 1998.
5. *News Letter*, January 10, 1998.
6. *News Letter*, January 10, 1998.
7. *Irish News*, January 10, 1998.
8. *Irish Times*, January 10, 1998.
9. "Conclusion of the Governments on the Position of the Ulster Democratic Party in the Talks," January 23, 1998.
10. *Irish Independent*, February 3, 1998.
11. *Belfast Telegraph*, February 10, 1998.
12. *The Times*, February 11, 1998.
13. *Irish News*, February 13, 1998.
14. "Conclusion of the Governments on the Position of Sinn Fein in the Talks," February 20, 1998.

CHAPTER 15

1. Transcript of press conference held at Stormont, March 25, 1998.
2. *Irish News*, March 28, 1998.
3. Transcript of press conference at Stormont, April 3, 1998.
4. *News Letter*, April 4, 1998.

5. *Irish News*, April 4, 1998.

6. "A New Framework for Agreement," February 1995.

7. *News Letter*, April 8, 1998.

8. Documentary by BBC Northern Ireland, "The Hand of History."

9. Ibid.

10. *Guardian*, April 9, 1998.

11. "Agreement Reached in the Multi-Party Negotiations," April 10, 1998, Strand Two, paragraph 13.

12. "Agreement Reached in the Multi-Party Negotiations," April 10, 1998, Declaration of Support, paragraph 4.

13. "Agreement Reached in the Multi-Party Negotiations," April 10, 1998, Strand One, paragraph 5 (d).

14. *Irish News*, April 10, 1998; *Times* of London, April 10, 1998.

PERMISSIONS ACKNOWLEDGMENTS

Grateful acknowledgment is made to the following for permission to reprint previously published material:

An Phoblacht/Republican News: Excerpt from an interview with an IRA spokesperson regarding the Mitchell Principles (*An Phoblacht/Republican News,* September 11, 1997). Reprinted by permission.

BBC: Excerpt from a BBC interview with David Trimble from the program "The Hand of History." Reprinted by permission of the BBC (British Broadcasting Corporation), London.

Financial Times: Excerpt from "Concentrating Irish Minds" (*Financial Times,* London, April 3, 1998). Reprinted by permission.

The Guardian: Excerpt from "The Bomb Made Headline News Across the United Kingdom and Ireland" by John Mullin (*The Guardian,* London, September 17, 1997), copyright © by *The Guardian.* Reprinted by permission.

Irish Independent: Excerpt from "Unholy War Threat Raises North Tension" by David McKittrick (*Irish Independent,* Dublin, February 3, 1998). Reprinted by permission.

The Irish News: Excerpt from "Setback as Mitchell Delays Key Document" by William Graham (*The Irish News,* Belfast, April 4, 1998). Reprinted by permission.

The Irish Times: Excerpt from article on "Strand Two" (*The Irish Times,* Dublin, April 2, 1998). Reprinted by permission.

News International Syndication: Excerpt from "Sinn Fein Will Accept Interim Peace Accords" by Martin Fletcher (*The Times,* London, July 22, 1997), excerpt from "Wright's Death Will Not Kill Off Dissident Group" by Martin Fletcher (*The Times,* London, December 29, 1997), excerpt from "Cease-fire in Balance after IRA Killings" by Martin Fletcher (*The Times,* London, February 11, 1998), © copyright 1997, 1998 by Times Newspapers Limited, London. Reprinted by permission.

News Letter: Excerpts from four articles (*News Letter,* Belfast, July 9, 1996, December 17, 1997, January 7, 1998, and January 10, 1998). Reprinted by permission.

GEORGE MITCHELL served as Senator from Maine from 1980 to 1995, the last six years as Majority Leader. Prior to that he served as U.S. Attorney for Maine and as a United States District Court Judge. Since leaving the Senate, in addition to chairing the Northern Ireland peace talks he has served as Chairman of the International Crisis Group, a nonprofit organization dedicated to the prevention of crises in international affairs; Chairman of the National Health Care Commission; Chairman of the Ethics Committee of the U.S. Olympic Committee; and chairman of the commission investigating allegations of corruption in the Olympic bid process. Senator Mitchell is married to the former Heather MacLachlan and they have one child, Andrew.

A NOTE ON THE TYPE

THIS BOOK was set in Janson, a typeface long thought to have been made by the Dutchman Anton Janson, who was a practicing typefounder in Leipzig during the years 1668–1687. However, it has been conclusively demonstrated that these types are actually the work of Nicholas Kis (1650–1702), a Hungarian, who most probably learned his trade from the master Dutch typefounder Dirk Voskens. The type is an excellent example of the influential and sturdy Dutch types that prevailed in England up to the time William Caslon (1692–1766) developed his own incomparable designs from them.

Composed by North Market Street Graphics,
Lancaster, Pennsylvania
Printed and bound by R. R. Donnelley & Sons,
Harrisonburg, Virginia
Designed by Virginia Tan